Windsor Ablaze!

The Windsor Castle Fire and Restoration

Alexandra Brown and Charles Chapman

The Lutterworth Press

The Lutterworth Press
P.O. Box 60
Cambridge
CB1 2NT

www.lutterworth.com
publishing@lutterworth.com

First Published in 2007

ISBN: 978 0 7188 3082 3

British Library Cataloguing in Publication Data
A catalogue record is available from the British Library

Picture Acknowledgements:
With grateful thanks to the following photo & illustration sources:
Charles Chapman: pp. 6, 8, 9, 25, 26, 32, 34, 35, 36 -45, 47-62, 6;
Alamy: pp. 4, 11 and front cover;
PA: pp. 13, 16, 17, 24, 30 (upper), 33;
R.L Day: pp. 21, 22, 27, 63;
The Royal Collection: p. 19 and back cover;
Giles Downes (Sidell Gibson): p. 28, 29, 30 (lower), 31, 46

Printed in the United Kingdom by
speedworks, Peterborough

Contents

Introduction

One of the greatest fires in the history of England erupted at Windsor Castle on 20 November 1992, Queen Elizabeth II's 45th wedding anniversary. Five years later, the Queen feted those who worked on the restoration as part of her 50th Wedding Anniversary celebrations. The image of that famous crenellated outline engulfed in flames is emblazoned in the collective memories of television viewers around the world. From the woeful charred ruins rose a rebuilding programme unequalled in the twentieth century and a process that permanently changed the modern British monarchy. Not every nation possesses the will, along with the skill, to restore a complex mediaeval fortress and palace. This is the story of that spectacular fire and the herculean task of restoration that it prompted, a part of the Castle's architectural history that will endure as a testimony to twentieth century British craftsmanship and a legacy for the future.

Ten years on, a new chapter has been written for Windsor Castle and for its monarchy. As the damaged Castle rose once again, so too did this monarchy enjoy a resurrection from the *annus horribilis* of 1992. A triumphant and popular Queen Elizabeth II, whose reign has extended over 55 years into the twenty-first century, celebrates 60 years of marriage, the longest of any British monarch in history, on the 10th anniversary of the completion of Windsor Castle's magnificent restoration.

20 November 1992, the
Castle Ablaze

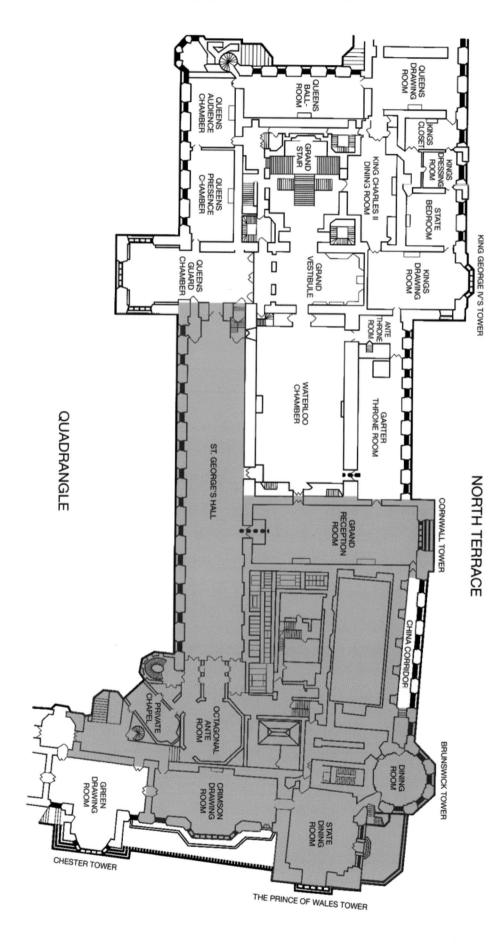

Castle Fire Illustration. Area of the State Apartments that were damaged by the 1992 fire before successful containment.

1
The History

Windsor Castle is the oldest royal residence in continuous use in the world. This living, working Castle, covering 13 acres, is a fortress, a royal residential palace for the Queen of England, an important church, and the dwellings and livelihood of many. Although its skyline of battlements, turrets and signature Round Tower is instantly recognised throughout the world, the Castle as we know it is an amalgam of architecture created for successive monarchs and reflects the architectural history of the nation.

The name Windsor derives from the old English word windlesora meaning 'river bank with a windlass'. Built on the only defendable site in this part of the Thames Valley by William the Conqueror, Windsor Castle was one of a network of defensive fortresses centred on the Tower of London. In 1110, William's son, Henry I, established the Castle as a residence fitting for his court, and the town grew below. Henry II, grandson of the conqueror, replaced the Castle's wooden walls with the more impenetrable stone. During the reign of King John, the Castle was besieged by land barons. After they had forced him to sign the historic Magna Carta in nearby Runnymede in 1215, the king tried to have the agreements annulled. In retaliation in 1216, the barons laid siege to the Castle once more .

Edward III, born in Windsor, founded the College of St George and the Order of the Garter on 23 April, 1348. Modelled after the tales of King Arthur's Round Table, it is the senior English order of chivalry. The original 26 members formed two groups, led respectively by the King and the Black Prince. The ceremony, including the procession of monarch and knights in dark blue robes survives to the present, while

The Garter Throne, dating from the time of Edward III (1327-1377), founder of the Most Noble Order of the Garter, the senior order of chivalry in England.

the Castle itself reflects Edward's ideal of Christian chivalric monarchy. St George's Chapel was built by Edward IV in 1475 as the spiritual home of the Order of the Garter. Henry VIII completed the Chapel and added the Great Gateway to the Lower Ward, an impressive entrance still used by visitors.

The Castle fortress played a major role in the English Civil War. In 1642 parliamentary troops captured Windsor establishing it as the military headquarters of Cromwell's New Model Army. It suffered neglect, its treasures looted by underpaid soldiers. Charles 1 was imprisoned here for a month.

Charles II, returning from exile in 1660, saw Windsor as a symbol of monarchy. He reinstated the Garter Ceremony, abandoned during the Commonwealth and commissioned Hugh May to re-create its role as a royal palace while keeping its medieval look. In the elaborate fashion of the day, baroque state apartments were added and the Italian painter Antonio Verrio covered May's ceilings with heroes, goddesses and the Black Prince's victory processions. It was during this period that Samuel Pepys described Windsor as 'the most romantique castle there is in the world'. Charles also laid out the Long Walk, the three-mile avenue leading to the Great Park.

George III loved the Castle and the adjoining Great Park and made minor changes to accommodate family life. In his last years, when becoming increasingly incapacitated by mental illness, it was to Windsor that he was confined.

In 1820, George IV, after nine years as Prince Regent, became king. An aesthete whose taste defined 'Regency' art, architecture and furniture, his short reign had a major impact on the re-design of Windsor Castle. A Francophile, he embarked on an ambitious royal palace building programme, turning Buckingham House into Buckingham Palace, the seat of the monarchy in London, and reconstructing Windsor Castle as his 'Versailles' in the country. He revamped the State Apartments, creating the elegant Crimson and Green Drawing Rooms as a showcase for the royal art and furniture collection and a Grand Reception Room richly decorated in Gobelins Tapestry and Louis XV panelling. Sir Jeffrey Wyattville was commissioned to remodel the Castle. In recreating St. George's Hall in Gothic revival style, Wyattville left a huge void between its flat decorated ceiling and the rooftop – an enormous fire trap that

enabled the fire of 1992 to spread so rapidly. Completing the medieval look, the Garter Knight heraldic shields were placed on the ceiling of St. George's Hall, covering Verrio's baroque frescoes. Ornate plaster, elaborate gilt-work and rich panelling were all hallmarks of Wyattville's interior design. In addition to the grand royal interiors, he created the romantic exterior. He constructed the high, octagonal Brunswick Tower to anchor the northeast corner, erected the long Cornwall Tower above the Grand Reception Room, and doubled the height of the Round Tower, creating the instantly recognisable signature look of the Castle. George IV's embellishments were to become the focal point of the 1992 fire.

Queen Victoria preferred Windsor Castle to London. She and Prince Albert and their large family enjoyed country pursuits in Windsor Great Park. During her reign, a stone gothic-style Grand Staircase decorated with Henry VIII's armour was created in the State Apartments and a new Private Chapel was built – in which the Great Fire of 1992 had its origins.

With the reign of Elizabeth II, Windsor came into its own as both Palace and family home. The Queen (then Princess Elizabeth) and her sister Princess Margaret were sent for safety here during World War II, along with the Crown Jewels. The Queen is often in residence, her standard flying from the Round Tower. The vast fire of 1992 provided an unforeseen opportunity to make her impact on the architecture of the Castle.

St George's Chapel in the Lower Ward of the Castle. The Chapel was founded in 1475 as the spiritual home of the Order of the Garter.

2
The Great Fire of 1992

For anyone who lives with a historic building, fire is the greatest fear. The void above Wyattville's ceiling in St George's Hall was the worst fire hazard in Windsor Castle. A fire there was everyone's worst nightmare.
Prince Edward Windsor, the Earl of Wessex

In 1992, the section of Windsor Castle in the Upper Ward that housed the first-floor State Apartments was being refitted with new wiring and, ironically, a new fire prevention system in an ongoing modernization project known as the Kingsbury project. Situated between the sumptuous State Apartments and the enormous 55 metre (180 ft) long St George's Hall, the Private Chapel was being used as a way station for moving precious paintings and artefacts to outside storage as each room went through the renovation process. Work was to begin in St George's Hall, and paintings of various monarchs had been taken to the Private Chapel to join some 20 others that had been stored there for several months. No sprinklers were installed and the smoke detectors were not activated.

On 20 November, the 45th wedding anniversary of the Queen and Prince Philip, fire erupted. At about 11:15 a.m., picture specialists in the Private Chapel detected a faint smell of burning but dismissed it. At 11:20, a plumber on the roof noticed smoke coming from the roof voids of St George's Chapel. At 11:28, the art specialists saw flames at the top of a closed six-metre curtain covering the recessed sanctuary of the Private Chapel. The fire was beyond the reach of any fire extinguisher and was later thought to be from a 1000 watt quartz halogen lamp igniting the heavy material of the curtain. When workmen at the scene could not quench the fire with extinguishers, at 11:35 Windsor Castle Fire Brigade was called, and relayed the

news to Berkshire County Fire and Rescue Service – Windsor Castle was on fire! With flames spreading rapidly, the art specialists and workmen quickly removed the paintings from the Chapel, managing to escape as the burning curtain fell to the floor, igniting foam packing material and pieces of falling ceiling plaster. The Castle fire-fighting apparatus was two miles away in the Great Park disposing of hazardous chemicals. By the time it arrived at 11:41, the ceiling and roof of the chapel were already aflame. With its connections to the enormous void above St George's Hall to the west and the State Apartments to the east, the Private Chapel provided a perfect conduit. Aged materials and a soaring roof void ignited so fast and created such a safety hazard that eight minutes after arriving, the Fire Brigade had to withdraw, as the fire spread behind panelling.

The local Berkshire Fire crew, based in Windsor, was seven miles away on a familiarization tour in Ascot. Slough Fire and Rescue Service arrived at 11:44 with a water tender and at 11:55 the Windsor team arrived. Had Windsor been at their local station, their response time would have been in

Lighting the night sky, the Brunswick Tower erupts into flame as fire-fighters battle the blaze from the Grand Quadrangle. Later records proved that the temperature in the Brunswick Tower soared to an astonishing 820 degrees Centigrade or 1508 degrees Fahrenheit. Criss-crossed with tracks to prevent the fire engines from sinking, this was the hub of the fire fighting activities.

two minutes, not nineteen. When the first County fire crew arrived, it required a detailed map of the Castle grounds, held in the Windsor Castle fire Station for security purposes. Water hydrants could not be found as they had been concealed by gravel. The stone gateway to the North Terrace was too narrow to allow modern fire engines through, so the central Grand Quadrangle had to be used at the south wall, requiring tracks to be laid to prevent the fire engines from sinking into the lawn.

The fire meanwhile spread rapidly at roof level destroying the ceilings of St George's Hall and the Grand Reception Room and gutting the Private Chapel, the State Dining Room, the Crimson Drawing Room, the Green Drawing Room and other rooms in the northeast corner of the Castle. So hot did this fire burn that parts of the great Henry Willis organ in the Private Chapel and lead in the Castle roof melted and fell to the floor.

By 1:03 p.m. there were 36 fire engines, 250 firefighters, 25 officers and 31 water jets. Old timber, dry textiles and plaster walls and ceilings fed the flames which licked their way between crevices and wall spaces, spreading through five floors. Crews came from every force in Berkshire, helped by brigades from London, Surrey, Hampshire, Wiltshire, Oxfordshire and Buckinghamshire. Firefighters pumped over 7,000,000 litres of water into the Castle. Water soaked into the immense thickness of the mediaeval walls and vaults and was absorbed by organic materials (the wood and silk) used in the construction and decoration of the Castle. Rivers of water ran down the blackened walls, and twisted wood and metal were thrust up into the open space where the roof had once been. Two years after the fire, some bricks were still 80% saturated with water. Despite this, the fire was so intense that six weeks later, when the lead work in the Cornwall Tower was being stripped, sparks in the embers lit another fire.

As rapidly as the fire spread, so too did the word spread in the world's media and the streets of Windsor were soon gridlocked with news teams and their camera equipment. Sightseers and residents of Windsor gathered in the November cold to mourn the burning national monument and the focal point of tourism. Within the Castle grounds, the Women's Royal Voluntary Service worked around the clock to supply firefighters, police and volunteers with food and drink from local restaurants.

By early afternoon, it was apparent that millions of litres of water alone could not contain the blaze; the decision was made to implement fire stops, sacrificing the remaining scorched and smoke-damaged interior walls and ceilings. The exterior walls were safe because of their immense thickness. Stops were placed at the west side of the Grand Reception Room and at the end of the Grand Corridor. Holes were made in the ornate plaster of the Green and Crimson Drawing Room ceilings so any flames that travelled there could be detected and fought.

Richard L. Day, now retired, worked for 45 years as a book restorer in the Windsor Castle Library and for over 33 years as a fireman. He was second in command of the Windsor Castle Fire Brigade and was the first officer on the scene at the fire, leading a group of part-timers. He recalls:

> *I had always admired the Ceiling in the Green Drawing Room whilst waiting for my annual Christmas present from the Queen. Little did I know that one day we'd have to cut through that same ceiling. . . .*

Ten crews directed constant streams of water at the blaze. The strategy was working. At 3:30 p.m., David Harper, of the Berkshire Fire Services, held a press conference declaring:

> *The fire is now controlled. But you must remember that there is a difference between controlled and extinguished. It isn't going anywhere. What you are seeing is as bad as it is going to get. It won't spread. It might consume where it is at the moment.*

With flames lighting the night sky as the world watched on live television, the fire burned continuously for 15 hours, generating a restoration cost of £2.3 million for every hour the fire lasted, or £38 000 per minute. At the apex of the fire, the temperature at the foot of the Brunswick Tower, which erupted in Vesuvius-like flames, reached 820°C (1508° F). Spectacular and theatrical as this sight was, the ignition of the Brunswick Tower's interior was the signal to the firefighters that the fire had turned and that their strategy was a success. Pushing the fire before them from the southwest, they knew it would vent both here and in the Prince of Wales Tower.

To combat the huge blaze, a total of 44 fire engines and 841 sets of breathing cylinders were used by firefighters – each breathing set lasting 20-25 minutes. By the end of this inferno, 105 rooms, including nine of the finest rooms in the State Apartments, or nearly one-fifth of Windsor Castle were damaged or destroyed; in round figures, approximately 9000 square meters. From the smoldering ashes of this terrible destruction rose a salvage and restoration process unprecedented in its ambitions and a historic undertaking of immense proportions.

Following pages: An aerial view of Windsor Castle illustrates the astonishing extent of the damage to the roof caused by the fire.

WINDSOR CASTLE FIRE TIMETABLE

11:15 Faint smell of burning detected in The Private Chapel

11:20 Plumber on roof sees smoke coming from the vents on the roof of St.George's Hall

11:35 Call logged at Windsor Castle Fire Brigade. part time firefighters contacted. Windsor Castle fire siren sounds.

11:41 Windsor Castle Fire Brigade arrives. The ceiling and roof of the Private Chapel are already aflame.

11:44 The first Fire engines arrive from Slough with water tender ladder. The call goes out to 'make pumps 10 '(a request for ten more fire engines).

11:55 Windsor Fire Engines arrive from Ascot

12:04 Fire spreading rapidly in the roof of St George's Hall. More breathing apparatus requested.

12:12 The call goes out to 'make pumps 20'

13:03 Request to "make pumps 25'

13:30 Fire Break established in the Green Drawing Room; fire crews begin to bring fire under control

14:33 Fire Breaks established at Chester Tower & Clock Tower

15:30 Fire officers announce that the fire is surrounded; floors within Brunswick Tower collapse.

18:30 With its windows backlit by fire, orange flames are seen shooting from the top of the Brunswick Tower.

20:00 Blaze is said to be brought under control

23:03 Message sent that no further appliances are needed.

23:30 Small pockets of flame continue to burn in the Castle

Saturday 2:30 am Fire is extinguished.

3
Salvage

Raging fire itself was not the only drama at Windsor
Castle that day. Within minutes of the start of the fire, an
immense operation to rescue the Castle's treasures was
mounted. While firemen combated the fire from the Great
Quadrangle, rescue was simultaneously taking place there
and at Engine Court. Shortly after arrival at the Castle, the
commanding officer of the Berkshire Fire Brigade ordered
a complete evacuation of the contents of the Upper Ward.
If the fire spread westwards into the splendidly furnished
staterooms, south into the private apartments of the Queen,
or north into the Library and Print room, the damage would
be incalculable.

Although fortune smiled rarely that day, it did put in a
token appearance. Despite it being a grey November day,
there was no rain and the Great Quadrangle was smoke-
free due to the prevailing winds – essential for removing the
furniture and fine art collections from danger. A squadron
of removal vans had arrived as part of a pre-determined
response that was implemented as soon as the alarm was
raised. The commander of the Windsor Fire Brigade soon
realised that, in the face of such a huge fire, his 25-man
salvage squad was completely inadequate. Windsor is a
garrison town with two barracks, Combermere and Victoria,
the latter just down the road from the Castle, to which the
guard return daily. A request went out for the assistance of
the Army's manpower plus as many Bedford vans as they
could spare. Staff drafted from different walks of life, and
even Prince Andrew, joined the army, firemen and the police
in a brilliant and well-coordinated salvage process.

A vast and important part of The Royal Collection's

The Crimson Drawing Room floor miraculously held despite meters of scorched and sodden debris from the collapsed ceiling and roof. 80% of the silk panelling was destroyed.

finest treasures were on display or kept in Windsor Castle. Assembled throughout the rooms were works of art of all kinds – Old Masters, drawings, sculptures, miniatures, furniture, ceramics, silver and gold plate, prints, books, manuscripts, arms and armour, gems, clocks, glass and tapestries, porcelain, Dutch, Italian and English pictures, collections of Fabergé. The Kingsbury modernisation project was a rolling one. While paintings and tapestries had been removed from St George's Hall that day preparatory to work, others such as those in the Grand Drawing Room had been returned as work was completed. In the face of such a formidable conflagration, immediate evacuation of priceless treasures became a priority. Although there were no suits of armour or paintings in St George's Hall at the time, it took 40 soldiers to roll and remove the two ton carpet which had to be removed in step. An eyewitness reports that only four were out of step. From there, the rug was marched to the Riding School in the Royal Mews and placed on wooden palettes for air circulation, all seams carefully arranged to ensure that they would dry straight. Enormous paintings had to be removed from the Waterloo Chamber, revealing the wall drawings from pantomime performances for the Princesses Elizabeth and Margaret during the war years. The Grand Reception Room held tapestries in huge picture frames with hidden doors to other rooms. The Windsor Castle Fire Brigade also played the role of pathfinders through many hidden doorways and passages, leading other firemen to the seat of the fire. Some tapestries were velcroed; some had grommets. Each type of fastening opened in a different direction and had to be carefully stripped and removed. The enormous Canalettos – which were on steel shafts – had to be cut away before they could be removed. From darkened rooms smelling of smoke, the Lawrences from the Waterloo Chamber, the Rubens, the Van Dykes, were all removed by the Windsor Fire Brigade, who wore breathing apparatus, under the direction of members of The Royal Collection. It took four men just to remove the mattress from Napoleon III's bed. In the Garter Room, where the Queen receives her Garter Knights on Garter Day, firemen pulled suits of armour from the horses as damage limitation.

During this heroic rescue operation, there was drama within drama like a set of Russian dolls. In the Royal Library, an urgent evacuation operation was underway. The Library is located in a first floor suite of rooms adjoining the State Apartments on the north side of the Upper Ward, which also houses a bookbindery and a museum. Before they could be damaged by fire, water or smoke, priceless books and treasures had to be evacuated. These included: fifteenth century illuminated manuscripts, such as the Sobieski Book of Hours; a collection of oriental manuscripts that included the Shahnama epic of 1648 chronicling the deeds of the kings of ancient Persia; original sovereigns' manuscripts; literary manuscripts of Dickens, Byron, Masefield, Hardy

and Ted Hughes, among others; some of the earliest Western printed books including The Mainz Psalter, the second book to be printed of movable type (1457) and four books printed by William Caxton, including one of his famed editions of Aesop's Fables; a collection of fine bindings throughout the ages; clocks; coins; and other museum pieces. The Print Room holds collections of Old Masters drawings, watercolours and prints, including 750 Da Vinci Drawings. Everything had to go . . . and fast. Smoke could do as much damage as fire. Relay lines were formed down the circular staircase by members of the Royal Household, the Army, Ghurkas, who were on guard duty at the time, resident Military Knights and their wives, and policemen. It took almost six hours to completely remove the collection and, when the time came, seven and a half months to put it back in order. Items were removed as indicated in the Salvage List, a well-developed plan for such an event, catalogued by fluorescent labels according to value, and stored in the safety of the Norman Tower. Every removal lorry had a policeman accompanying the driver.

By 1pm, the salvage operation was in full swing. Local police, the military & resident volunteers assisted the 25 man salvage squad in removing priceless treasures to Engine Court. In the background, portfolios are passed along the relay line from the Royal Library to the removal vans.

The Carpet in St George's Hall is the longest carpet of the Royal Palaces and one of the largest in the world. It took 40 men to roll and remove to safety while the fire raged.

Scattered around the Castle lawns under a pewter sky were millions of pounds worth of priceless treasures – picture frames leaning against marble tables, an urn here, a gilt chair there. Only one picture was lost early on to the fire in the Private Chapel. Nothing was reported missing.

At the end of this incredible salvage operation, where everything movable was dispatched with as much care as haste, the only pieces left to the flames were those which were too heavy, too difficult to reach, or too cumbersome for rescue workers. These included: the giant Malachite Urn given to Queen Victoria by Tsar Nicholas I; the chandeliers in the Grand Reception Room and in the Crimson and Green Drawing Rooms; and one table. Of these items, only the table was destroyed, the others requiring extensive restoration.

4

The Royals and the Restoration

Windsor Castle is more than just a castle to Queen Elizabeth II; it is also a private home. Devastation here went to the heart of her Monarchy and family life. As a place where she spent many happy years growing up, the Castle had always loomed large in the Queen's affections and remains one of her favourite residences. During World War II, the Queen and her sister Princess Margaret were evacuated to Windsor Castle and often joined in with the life of the town beyond the Castle walls. Childhood pantomimes were performed in the Waterloo Chamber and, during the war years, Princess Elizabeth joined the local girl guides and Auxiliary Territorial Service (ATS). When she became Queen in 1952, one of her first acts was to announce that Windsor Castle would serve as her weekend retreat. As a royal residence, the Castle also plays an important part in receiving and entertaining Heads of State. Every June, the Queen, as Sovereign, presides over the Royal Order of the Garter services – Britain's highest and most prestigious chivalric Order - which includes assembly in St George's Hall, lunch in the Waterloo Chamber, services in St George's Chapel, and an investiture ceremony for any new Garter Knight. Garter Day sets the Royal Calendar for the year and is immediately followed by Royal Ascot Week, officially attended by the Queen and the Royal Family, who set out from Windsor Castle throughout the five day sporting and social event.

On the afternoon of 20 November, Queen Elizabeth arrived from Buckingham Palace to survey her still burning and smoking Castle, a sombre figure in rain mac and wellies, whose stricken face said it all. She toured the now-stripped Waterloo Chamber, inspected the evacuated furnishings in the Castle grounds, and was kept informed of the progress of

The Queen surveys the
destruction caused by
fire, smoke and water
in what remains of St
George's Hall.

the firefighting. She also had to attend to the removal of her
own personal possessions to ensure their safety should the fire
spread south to her apartments. To the Queen, this fire was a
huge personal tragedy. Not only was her home in the process
of being destroyed, but one of the nation's great icons was
imperilled. As Sovereign, the Queen's strong sense of duty has
been her guiding force. To have this destruction on her watch
was a cruel blow that struck deeply. It was to get worse.

While the citizens of Great Britain might have been
expected to sympathize and stand by a visibly forlorn Queen,
they did no such thing. This was no kind and grateful nation.
The Royal Household had taken over responsibility for the
royal residences from the Property Services Agency in 1991,
and were held accountable. The subject of restoring the Castle
immediately embroiled the Royal Family in controversy. The
cost was estimated at £42 million and the Heritage Secretary,
Peter Brook, during a visit to the charred Castle, announced
that the Government would bear the full cost of rebuilding,
including ornamental plasterwork on the ceilings, repairs to
the wooden floors, and any structural repair work. There was

uproar in the tabloid press. Britain was in the grip of a recession and the people were in no mood to see their taxes spent on a royal residence while thousands of households were threatened by foreclosure and negative equity. Furthermore, reports of disastrous cuts began appearing in the press. Two days after the fire *The Sunday Times* carried news of royal purse-cutting that caused delay as Windsor Castle burned. The Windsor Castle Fire Brigade had been reduced by layoffs and the decision to scale down the response vehicles to one customized van and a pump only capable of generating a water pressure of 250 lb per square inch. In those first crucial moments, it was reported, they had insufficient water pressure to reach the flames. Also, the backup system from Romney Lock, providing 1200 gallons of water, had been closed by the Royal Household in January, 1992, when they took over from the Department of Environment. It was only brought into action 90 minutes after the blaze had started and begun consuming St George's Hall.

Gold coin commemorating the restoration of Windsor Castle awarded by Queen Elizabeth to those who worked so tirelessly on its successful completion.

Worse, Windsor Castle was discovered to be uninsured. While the government's Property Services Agency had been responsible for the royal residences, it had never insured the building or its fixtures and fittings. When the Royal Household took over in 1991, it made no changes to this arrangement. No insurance policies were in place to cover the buildings, the Royal Family's Private Collection, or personal possessions (the Royal Collection had its own insurance). Arguments erupted as to which fixtures and fittings the Government would cover and what was private. The Junior Minister Robert Key responded that payment of government money to cover private losses was unlikely, adding: "I think that the Royal Family would probably face the bill from their own resources."

On Saturday night, Labour MPs complained of the tax burden for reconstruction, contrasting it with the Queen's privileged tax position. Tony Benn M.P. asked if the tax would come from the homeless. The chairman of the Public Accounts Select Committee suggested a Select Committee to scrutinize the Queen's Civil List and whether she should pay income tax; Alan Williams, member of the all-party Committee added that the Royal Exemption covers Inheritance Tax and Capital Gains Tax as well as Income Tax, stating: " It is unacceptable that existing taxpayers should be required to meet major capital

A smiling Queen Elizabeth II and Prince Philip during the annual Garter Procession.

losses such as the fire while royals enjoy exclusive benefit of all gains. The fire may be the catalyst." Indeed it was.

When Parliament convened on 23 November, there was no equivocation and no doubt where blame was to be directed: "Responsibility for fire safety at Windsor Castle and all occupied royal residences has been vested in the Royal Household since 1 April 1991." In fact, the public was growing considerably weary of the Royal Family that year. They were not at the height of popularity at the time of the fire. Four days after the fire, at a lunch in London's Guildhall, obviously stung by public reaction to events at Windsor, the Queen famously referred to 1992 as her "*annus horribilis*". The Castle fire was seen as the final blow in a year when the marital problems of her children had titillated the international media, compromising her own lifetime of personal rectitude. The year had been memorable. Andrew Morton had published his best-selling book on Princess Diana, revealing an unflattering picture of the Queen's eldest son, and life within royal walls. Her second son Prince Andrew officially separated from his wife Sarah Ferguson, who was caught that summer in the tabloid media romping topless in the Riviera in the company of her Texan financial advisor with the royal grandchildren in tow. Even the relatively staid Princess Anne was involved in divorce. In her speech at the Guildhall, an unusually defensive Queen declared of the fire:

I dare say that history will take a more moderate view that of contemporary commentators. Distance is well known to lend enchantment even to the less attractive views. After all it has the inestimable advantage of hindsight. But it can also lend an extra dimension to judgment giving it a leavening of moderation and compassion – even of wisdom – that is sometimes lacking in the reactions of those whose task in life is to offer instant opinions on all things great and small . . . we are all part of the same fabric of our national society and that scrutiny, by one part of another can be just as effective if it is made with a touch of gentleness, good humour and understanding.

Needless to say, this had no effect on the infamous British media – now in full cry. But while the press continued to

Opposite: Restoration in process at St George's Hall following the erection of a new permanent roof.

give instant opinions, there was no question about the royal resolve to restore Windsor Castle...and fast! At that time there were a number of minor royals who were still being paid out of the Exchequer. On the Thursday following the fire, the Queen agreed to limit the members of The Royal Family paid from the public purse to only three – herself, the Duke of Edinburgh and the Queen Mother. To quell criticism that might delay restoration, the notoriously frugal Queen agreed to pay income tax for the first time in the history of the monarchy. From the beginning, when the Duke of York was on the salvage line passing treasures hand-to-hand and reporting on the progress of the fire to the press every hour, the Royal Family took an active part in the restoration process, with Prince Philip chairing the Restoration Committee, and the

The armoured mounted statue of the King's Champion atop the balcony of the spectacular East Screen built at St. George's Hall to replace the one vaporized by the fire. The carved central doors lead to the octagonal Lantern Lobby and the State Apartments.

Prince of Wales the Design Committee. To help pay for the reconstruction, the Queen opened Buckingham Palace to the public for the first time and Windsor Castle started charging admission.

The astonishing task of restoring Windsor Castle was eventually completed at a cost of £37 million – under budget and ahead of schedule. (For anyone living in England, this is nothing short of miraculous.) Revenue from admissions to the Buckingham Palace Staterooms and the public rooms and precincts of Windsor Castle paid 70% of the total bill. The rest was paid from savings from the annual Grant-in-Aid for the maintenance and upkeep of the occupied Royal Palaces. Thus the restoration was completed at no extra cost to the taxpayer; a triumph of the resolve of Queen Elizabeth II and her family.

5
The Great Restoration, 1992–1997

The five-year rebuilding of Windsor Castle was the biggest restoration project ever undertaken in Britain and the biggest royal building project of the twentieth century. It began the day after the fire and galvanized an unprecedented coalition of English Heritage, the Royal Household, The Royal Collection, the then Department of National Heritage, the Royal Fine Arts Commission, and a collection of artisans the modern world had never before seen assembled. The decision was made to rebuild and restore the Castle better than ever, and to accomplish this task using all British craftsmen and women.

The majority of the materials used in the renovation also came from Britain. Much of the timber came from the Crown's own Windsor Great Park and the great trusses of green oak used to create the beams of the new St George's Hall came from Herefordshire. The reconstruction comprised the largest amount of gilding in a single job undertaken in the twentieth century and the largest order for silks and passementerie (curtain ornamentation such as hangings, fringes and tassels) in living memory. The only piece of work which went outside Britain was part of the tassel order for the curtains in the Green and Crimson Drawing Rooms which went to Portugal; the largest order for tassels ever.

The restoration period saw employment of 200 contractors/sub-contractors, 19 firms of consultants and 5000 workers. Approximately 12000 deliveries were made to the site and over 300 oak trees were harvested in the reconstruction of St George's Hall alone.

The restoration process was divided into four phases. During the first phase of debris clearance and temporary roof building, 7000 dustbins were filled. Salvage pieces were

Carved unicorns flank the figure of the King's Champion on the balcony of the East Screen of St. George's Hall.

numbered and placed into 2000 breadbaskets. Temporary roofing was supported by 45 km (28 miles) of scaffolding and, at one stage, 121 km (75 miles) of scaffolding was erected. End to end this would reach from London to Dover or from London to Windsor and back again.

Once the best approach to each room had been determined, a combination of dehumidification, air circulation and natural ventilation was utilized to remove water from the building. Because of the havoc wreaked by fire and water, it was necessary to strip damaged areas right back to bare stonework. During George IV's reign and its major refurbishment, it was the fashion to cover existing architecture with plaster in a Gothic revival style. The fire partially burned this layer off revealing hitherto unknown original designs dating back to the Middle Ages. These revelations have led to a deepened understanding of the Castle's unique history.

New archaeological finds include: fragments of Antonio Verrio's seventeenth century murals for Charles II in St George's Hall; one of Britain's earliest windows with its original glass which had long ago been bricked up; grooves for the portcullis of the gatehouse to the historic kitchen

courtyard dating from the fourteenth century; a long forgotten 42 metre mediaeval well reaching down to the level of the Thames which supplied the kitchen with water; fourteenth century timbers in the kitchen Roof Lantern and even a fourteenth century cess pit which gave archaeologists a field day and enabled them to learn about people's diets and food preparation in the Middle Ages.

In early November 1992, English Heritage had just completed three years of investigative work on the Round Tower in conjunction with a programme of rebuilding the foundations which had been undermined as a result of

The Brunswick Tower was at the apex of the Great Fire of 1992 when its floors collapsed and flames soared up through the roof. Fully restored, it houses the Octagonal Dining Room.

Wyattville's heightening of the exterior walls in the nineteenth century. Called back the day after the fire to share their archaeological knowledge of the Castle, they had something else to offer – experience in reconstructing both Uppark Hall and Hampton Court Palace after their fires. These projects served as inspiration for the Windsor restoration. Valuable lessons in salvage, clearance and reconstruction had been learned and were welcomed and implemented immediately. These lessons, combined with the Royal Household's determination to bring this work within budget, meant that almost every piece of devastated material was repaired, restored or brought back. Because the Royal Household chose to restore so much of the original material, plaster fragments and charred wooden beams were stored in the Old Mushroom Complex agricultural buildings in Windsor Great Park, using indexed crates with pre-determined grid references for each room. Every nail was kept. Old balustrades were sent to be measured for reconstruction.

The ground floor was saturated with water, which was still dripping from drenched silken walls and twisted metal. In some places, the debris was two metres deep. Above St George's Hall, the Castle was open to the sky in a wintry British November. The priority was to build a temporary roof to keep out rain but provide enough air to circulate to prevent rot. Dehumidifiers had to be utilised for months. Some plaster took six months to dry. Wood was taken away to dustbins for storage. Steel girders were needed to strengthen the Brunswick Tower. St George's Hall had lost its ceiling and roof. The once elegant Green and Crimson Drawing Rooms were in ruins from fire and smoke and were water-filled. In the Crimson Drawing Room, the crystal chandelier was still hanging but broken and damaged and 80% of the silk wall panelling had been destroyed. The Malachite Urn in the Grand Reception Room, too large to be removed, survived the fire but required extensive restoration. The baroque ceiling of the Reception Room collapsed.

But exactly how do you restore a heritage monument that is also a working Castle and part of the panoply of State? Restore the damaged rooms to how they looked the day before the fire or to how they looked when originally commissioned? What about that dangerous roof void in St George's Chapel? And what to do with the newly revealed structures that appeared after the

nineteenth century plaster was removed? Cover them up again? What was the standard here? Anyone with experience in British planning authorities, listed buildings and committee work will appreciate what went on in meeting after meeting. English Heritage with its reverence for archaeological excavation and preservation was in no hurry to restore and reopen. The opportunity for scholarly interpretation was too tempting. The Royal Household, faced with a hard fought budget and criticism in the press, was driven towards an early completion. The Royal Collection wanted their treasures restored in the proper setting. The Queen and Prince Philip were determined to have their home back as soon as possible.

In the end, the overwhelming consideration was that Windsor Castle is a working Castle used for constitutional ceremonies, not a museum. It had to be restored to be functional and ceremonial, but clear opportunities also existed to make some desired changes. One thing all factions agreed on: Windsor Castle is an ancient monument and nothing less than the highest standards of workmanship would be countenanced. The recession, which had such an adverse effect on the public mood regarding financial responsibility for the Castle's ultimate repair, worked in their favour when it came to the restoration budget. Firms with little work in sight were willing to cut their

Plaster Modeller Miranda Carter carefully attends to the reconstruction of the cornice of the Grand Reception Room. Traditional techniques were used to recreate what was lost in the fire and restore what was salvaged.

The State Dining Room had to be reconstructed from photographic evidence and illustrations. Nothing remained after the fire.

costs in order to land the contract. They knew they would be paid. Another phenomenon working in the Royal Household's favour was what came to be known as 'the Windsor factor'. Craftsmen, consultants, construction and engineering firms perceived that being associated with the restoration of Windsor Castle would be beneficial for their firms in the future. And their workmanship and reputation would be on the line.

Often pilloried in the British press for his outspokenness, Prince Philip's leadership qualities included a decisive personality with a history of naval command and a no-nonsense attitude. Furthermore Windsor Castle was the Queen's and his family home. To ensure that there was no further delay, he took charge of the Restoration Committee; Prince Charles, with his well known interest in architecture, spearheaded the Design Committee. Final say on all decisions rested with the Queen.

Because the furnishings and collections had been successfully salvaged the day of the fire, most of the restoration work required after the drying out process was confined to walls, ceilings, floors and roofs, to include St George's Hall, the Grand Reception Room, the Green and Crimson Drawing Rooms, the Private Chapel and the Great Kitchen among

others. Reinforcement was needed for the Brunswick Tower.

Previous experience had taught English Heritage the importance of painstaking salvage to ensure historical reconstruction. From the beginning, they made it clear that before any engineers (and their boots) or mop up efforts were to get underway, their salvage experts were to systematically clear the floors. Combing assiduously through the debris over the course of months after the water was drained, English Heritage teams sifted 15000 fragments of plaster from the remains of various rooms, collecting them in 2000 indexed bread baskets. The restoration project at Hampton Court had helped to revive traditional crafts. Many master craftsmen who had worked with English Heritage in the 80s were drafted in at Windsor Castle. Using photographs from various sources as a guide, a skilled team of 30 plaster restorers painstakingly pieced together intricate designs. Master craftsmen cast moulds of plaster to exactly reproduce what couldn't be salvaged. Thousands of tiny shards of glass were gathered from five stateroom chandeliers, shattered when ceilings collapsed. Skilled glassworkers cleaned and polished them; top glassmakers faithfully reproduced the missing pieces from

The window of the Crimson Drawing Room looking out over the Grand Quadrangle. The nineteenth century window and wall had been cracked down the middle during the fire and had to be completely rebuilt.

The soaring ceiling of the Lantern Lobby built on the original site of the fire. No straight piece of wood was used.

photographic evidence. 900 blackened coats of arms were salvaged, repainted or authentically recreated from designs of the College of Heraldry.

Whether to restore or redesign the damaged rooms became a subject of continuing architectural controversy. Some saw an opportunity to add a completely modern touch to Windsor Castle. Others wanted a faithful return

Members of the international press get their first glimpse of the Grand Reception Room following restoration.

to the past. With an eye to quick completion and a set budget, Prince Philip's Restoration Committee made the decision to authentically restore most of the damaged State Apartments, including the Grand Reception Room and the Green and Crimson Drawing Rooms, all rooms in which the ornate furniture and treasures had been successfully saved. And to completely redesign six rooms including St George's Hall (which no one had liked much anyway) and the Private Chapel in which the fire had originated. Prince Charles' Design Committee also advocated the restoration of a fourteenth century Undercroft discovered under St George's Hall after the fire, now considered to be one of the greatest triumphs of the restoration. Although work had begun the day after the fire, The Royal Household assigned a Project Manager within five months who assembled a team of engineers, consultants and contractors representing the cream of the UK construction industry.

Redesign and The Triumph of St George's Hall

In response to the controversy raging in the architectural community, *Country Life* magazine had organised a national competition, albeit unofficial, for the redesign of St George's Hall. Designs ranged from a ceiling and roof with a transparent panel along the path of the Heathrow runway so planes could be seen gliding above, to one that allowed a meadow to

Opposite: The beautiful Stuart Stairwell with swirling bronze handrail leading from the Lantern Lobby balcony was created from the ruins of the Private Chapel.

grow among romantic ruins. None of the publicised designs met even the basic criteria of the Royal Household that form should follow function – in this case, the ceremonies of state. In the end, the Restoration Committee decided to remain faithful to the theme of successive reinterpretations of Gothic architecture that had characterised previous reconstructions of Windsor Castle, incorporating twentieth century interpretations and materials. The contract went to the firm of Sidell Gibson with Giles Downes as architect; a decision that was truly inspired.

By Spring of 1994, a permanent steel beamed roof was erected over the emptiness of St George's Hall, with fire retardant foam on the girders, and the time for interior work had arrived. At 55 metres (180 ft) long, it is the largest stateroom of the British monarchy. The secular counterpart to St George's Chapel, its purpose had always been celebration, its design that of a medieval banqueting hall.

The look of Wyattville's Hall was boxy and stunted with a flat plaster ceiling painted to look like wood. From Giles Downes, a stunningly redesigned St George's Hall rose, featuring a soaring Gothic ceiling three feet higher than before, crafted of wooden trusses from 352 Welsh Oak trees, felled and inserted green to dry and contract, with beams and dowel pegs crafted by hand. Starting from a lower point on the walls and rising to a central ridge almost 12 metres above the floor, 55 metres long and 9 metres wide, the effect is bold and dramatic – worthy of the highest medieval order. Completed in situ in September of 1996, it is the largest green oak structure built since the Middle Ages and the most complex since the sixteenth century, featuring the warmth of a hand made finish.

The colourful Garter shields of all the Knights of the Garter were authentically restored or reproduced according to the designs of the College of Heraldry and mounted on the ceiling. An index to the heraldry shields is set on the walls.

To complete the look, at the eastern end of the hall, where the screen and organ had disappeared, a new East screen appeared with a balcony bearing the armour of the King's Champion, an apt focal point of the room. Thus St George's

The Green Drawing Room was partially damaged during the fire and its ceiling cut as part of the fire control measures. Now magnificently restored, it has been added to the visitor route and is a great favourite.

Hall, the room worst hit by the fire of 1992, has been thrillingly redesigned and recreated better than ever.

Giles Downes next turned his attention to the new Lantern Lobby. This new Octagonal Chamber, created on the site of the old Private Chapel, was designed as an ante room to facilitate flow between St George's Hall and the Crimson and Green Drawing Rooms. With a stone floor depicting the Order of the Garter and eight beautifully fluted oak columns, it is a delicate and beautiful room. Surrounded as it is by thick

The splendid vaulted ceiling of St George's Hall designed by Giles Downes decorated with the shields of the Garter Knights.

walls and no windows, a soaring carved wooden Lantern atop a curved ceiling was constructed above them allowing natural light. With no straight section, each panel had to be laser cut, not sawn. Here, at the exact spot that a huge curtain met a hot spotlight to create history, an inscribed marble tablet was erected to commemorate the Fire of 1992.

In the new Private Chapel, now relocated next to the Lantern Lobby, with an intricate new ceiling of interlaced oak ribs, rose a stunning stained glass window based on a design by Prince Philip, a new organ, and a new altar designed by David Linley, son of Princess Margaret, the Queen's nephew. At the private dedication ceremony, the Queen and the Royal Family were joined by a small coterie of craftsmen and their families.

The Restored State Rooms

While creative redesign was the order of the day in St George's Hall, authentic restoration works were being carried out elsewhere. George IV, while often a figure of fun for his girth and opulent taste, was also one of England's greatest patrons.

His purchases enriched the Royal Collection. His patronage and donations added greatly to the collections of the British Museum and the National Gallery. More than just a testament to his regal taste, his rooms were designed as deliberate stage pieces in the national theatre of monarchical grandeur in an age when the great European dynasties were either being sidelined in affairs of state or falling to revolutionary fervour.

Restorers likened working on these rooms to assembling a massive jigsaw puzzle – piecing together crystal shards from the chandeliers, blasted malachite from the urn, fragments of plaster and filigree from the ceilings and walls. Aptly named and designed to impress, the Grand Reception Room was 12 metres tall, 9 metres wide, 30 metres long and opulently decorated in Rococo style. The huge ceiling, which collapsed in the fire, had to be completely recreated following extensive salvage. One year was spent working on the Grand Reception Room ceiling alone; 1022 sq. metres of gilding was used to faithfully restore the baroque details.

For the floor, which survived intact though waterlogged, the Royal Household implemented a brilliant cost cutting

The Crimson Drawing Room was restored exactly as it was before the fire. This and the Green Drawing Room are considered to be the finest examples of Regency Period decor.

measure. The huge oak floor was dried out, turned over, and restored. On the massive walls, the intricate Gobelins tapestry was cleaned, reframed and re-hung with one small difference. Shrunk in the drying process, it now has a four inch border around it. The Malachite Urn, successfully restored to its original nineteenth century condition, still dominates the room in regal splendour.

Considered the greatest examples of Regency period elegance, the French inspired Crimson and Green Drawing Rooms were masterfully restored. Around the door panels of these rooms, 63 intricately carved giltwood pieces called trophies – the finest woodcarvings of their kind in England – were recreated from photographs. In the Crimson Drawing Room, silk wall linings were reproduced, ornate plaster panels reinstalled – some new, some reconstructed – and painstakingly decorated in 24 ct. gilt. Crystal chandeliers were carefully reassembled, polished to lustre, and replaced. The beautiful ceilings of both rooms were restored so carefully in plaster and gilt that it is impossible to tell the new from the old, a testament to modern British craftsmanship. In all, 570 square metres of plaster work, the largest area of plaster work in the UK, were installed in Windsor Castle. Every piece of furniture in the Green and Crimson furniture was reupholstered.

In the two centuries after the grand furnishings were originally built for the Drawing Rooms, various renovations had replaced the material in wall panellings and curtains. Now that the settings to which they were being returned had been restored, there was an excellent opportunity to replace curtains and wall coverings, creating rooms more resplendent than they had been before the fire.

The veteran theatrical designer Pamela Lewis who had experience in redecorating palaces and a specialist in historically correct curtains, was hired. She was the perfect choice to restore the original theatricality of the rooms. Using paintings, photos and old drawings, beautiful silk damask panels were dyed for the Green and Crimson Drawing Room walls and for new curtains far more luxurious than before.

And, hidden among the ornate decorations, 750 new fire detectors were installed.

A portrait of King George VI displaying the blue garter of the Royal Order of the Garter is restored to the walls of the Crimson Drawing Room.

More Revelations

When much of the early nineteenth century interior design of the Castle was destroyed, fallen walls and ceilings and stripped plaster soon revealed lost and previously hidden medieval features. The damaged Castle provided unprecedented opportunities for historians and archaeologists.

The restoration of the Great Kitchen Roof is a great triumph, incorporating as it does some of the original thirteenth century beams discovered during the recovery process.

The Great Kitchen Roof

During the fire, the Great Kitchen of Windsor Castle lost its roof and ceiling which collapsed atop the 16 new ovens that had just been installed as part of the Kingsbury modernisation project. Although not part of the visitor experience, the kitchen is at the heart of ceremonial receptions and state entertainment at the Castle.

Previously believed to be no older than seventeenth century, the removal of the plaster following the fire laid bare a far richer history. The north wall of the Kitchen was found to be a twelfth century stone curtain wall with a great medieval fireplace set against it. In the thirteenth century, a stone kitchen was built on top of it. Prior to this discovery the oldest surviving royal kitchen was believed to be that at Hampton Court. Windsor's Great Kitchen is now known to be one of the oldest continuously used kitchens in the country.

The most striking feature of the Great Kitchen Roof is the roof lantern along most of its length allowing in daylight. Study of its timbers revealed thirteenth, fourteenth and fifteenth century components. English Heritage actually found sapwood in the fourteenth century timbers. Foundations dating back to the fourteenth century were also discovered. In later centuries, the kitchen was considered obsolete and was neglected. During Wyattville's time, it was restored again and became the heart of the royal kitchen complex with new fireplaces and chimney stacks.

In the Restoration process of 1992-1997, it was decided to authentically restore the Great Kitchen vaulted roof and its marvellous roof lantern. Although fitted with all modern appliances at its core, Windsor Castle's Great Kitchen was restored incorporating the reinforced medieval timbers in its striking roof with the great top lantern and elements of Wyattville's kitchen – the greatest example of a nineteenth century kitchen in Britain. Wyattville's massive kitchen tables and workbenches still survive, as well as long brass wall strips for hanging brass and copper kitchen implements.

The Undercroft
Many of the archaeological discoveries influenced the design of the reconstruction project. Blocked doorways sealed off for 150 years have been restored to use. It was at the Prince of Wales' insistence that the newly revealed Undercroft was restored. The restoration of the fourteenth century Undercroft is now considered one of the greatest triumphs of the twentieth-century restoration project. Located under St George's Hall, over time it had been subdivided into three separate bricked rooms during the reign of Charles II in the seventeenth century. Excavations also uncovered seventeenth century Purbeck stone and the threshold of a seventeenth century brick door with a gold coin from the reign of Edward IV set into the mortar, possibly serving as a charm. The long vaulted ground floor Undercroft, built by Edward IV to underpin his Great Hall, survived the fire in its entirety. The brick partition walls

were removed and the long room reunited under its vaulted roof. Restored, the fourteenth century Undercroft successfully recreates the feeling of a real medieval castle.

The fourteenth-century Undercroft was revealed under St George's Hall and restored at the insistence of Prince Charles' Design Committee.

Verrio's Paintings

During the seventeenth century, the Italian artist Antonio Verrio created an enormous 33.5 metre (110 ft) long fresco for the north wall of St George's Hall with life-size images of The Black Prince being greeted by his father Edward III. The centrepiece of his elaborate ceiling was a portrait of Charles II ascending to heaven. This rich baroque creation was thought to have been totally destroyed during Wyattville's construction.

When the plaster was removed after the fire, fragments of Verrio's work were, however, discovered at the top of the Hall. Although not enough remained to be restored, English Heritage was able to photograph the remnants, which were

The medieval Green Man carved on the plaster vault of the Stuart stairwell with oak leaves sprouting from his face is actually a portrait of architect Giles Downes. The sweeping balustrade leads to the Lantern Lobby balcony.

then carefully cleaned beforw being resealed under the plasterwork.

Amazingly enough, shortly after this discovery, an art dealer recognised the figure of Charles II at a continental auction. Painted on lath and plaster, this turned out to be the figure of Charles II from Verrio's ceiling which had been cut out and removed. (And presumably stolen, which raises questions of what else is out there!) The piece was purchased for The Royal Collection and is now part of the archives at Windsor.

6
The Restored Castle

The fire, damage and restoration of Windsor Castle has moved from tragedy to triumph in a modern mediaeval fairy tale that has ended happily. On 17 November 1997, a grateful Queen Elizabeth held a congratulatory dinner at the Castle for the craftsmen and women responsible for the remarkable restoration as part of her Golden Wedding Anniversary celebrations. On 20 November, the Queen and Prince Philip celebrated their Golden Wedding Anniversary with 600 guests at a glittering, renewed and restored Windsor Castle, five years to the day after the Fire. One month later, on 27 December, the newly restored rooms of the Castle were opened to the public.

Ten years later, visitors to these rooms still experience sensations not usually associated with heritage sites. The clean, freshly cut wood, the glint of bright gilt and the vibrant colours of new upholstery tantalize the senses. This is an unprecedented opportunity to experience the royal surroundings as they were when first commissioned centuries ago.

A post-fire review process opened up more rooms to public viewing than ever before, resulting in a restored Windsor Castle that is better than ever. In the State Apartments, St George's Hall and the Grand Reception Room have once again been included in the visitor route. For the first time, the Semi-State Rooms including the Green Drawing Room (view only), the Crimson Drawing Room, the State Dining Room, the Octagon Dining Room, the China Corridor and the Private Chapel have been opened to the public. The State Apartments are on view whenever the Castle is open except between 8 and 20 June to allow for preparations for the

This marble commemorative plaque now stands at the octagonal anteroom of the Lantern Lobby at the exact site where the Fire of 1992 originated.

Looking past the Moat Garden to the gateway of the Upper Ward.

annual investiture and ceremony of the Order of the Garter. Semi-State rooms remain open from October to March each year. The eastern end of the North Terrace overlooking the East Terrace Garden is open during August and September each year. A marble plaque in the octagonal anteroom of the Lantern Lobby commemorates the site where the fire originated in 1992.

Since completion of the restoration in 1997, Windsor Castle has once more taken its place in the ceremonial history of the nation and in the lives of the Royal Family. New royal occasions have placed Windsor Castle even more in the public eye. The Royal Wedding of Prince Edward and Sophie Rhys-Jones, the first prominent royal couple to be married in St George's Chapel at Windsor Castle in 95 years, took place on 19 June 1999 and attracted worldwide coverage. The streets of Windsor were once again swollen with international media and their equipment. The wedding event crowned a week of

pageantry and royalty that began with the Garter Ceremony, continued into the festivities and royal appearances of Royal Ascot Week, and climaxed in the Royal Wedding itself, set in "the most romantique castle there is in the world". After the wedding service, the royal newlyweds emerged from the Henry VIII Gate and into public view for a short carriage drive down Castle Hill and along High Street and Park Street, then back through the Cambridge Gate of Windsor Castle on the Long Walk for their wedding reception.

Prince Charles and Prince Andrew escorting their youngest brother Prince Edward to his wedding at St George's Chapel, the first prominent members of the Royal Family to be married there in 95 years.

Six years later, the wedding of Prince Charles and Camilla Parker Bowles took place on Saturday 9 April 2005, with a civil ceremony in the historic Windsor Guildhall, completed by Sir Christopher Wren in 1689, followed by a blessing by the Archbishop of Canterbury in St George's Chapel in Windsor Castle. This historic occasion, the celebration of the wedding of a divorced heir to the throne to a divorced woman in the same Castle where King Edward VIII abdicated in order to marry a divorced woman, was carried out with dignity and attended by streets full of wellwishers, despite what seemed a deliberate attempt on behalf of the media to heap their nuptials with scorn over the preceding weeks. Every glitch in the wedding couple's plans made headline news. The original plans to have the civil ceremony in Windsor Castle had to be changed because the Castle was not licensed to perform civil ceremonies. At the last minute, the date of the wedding had to be postponed for one day because of the death and funeral services of the Pope which Prince Charles was obliged to attend on behalf of his mother. The Service of Prayer and Dedication in St George's Chapel was attended by the Queen and the Duke of Edinburgh and other members of the Royal Family as well as Mrs Parker Bowles' family and guests and was carried live on television. Following the beautiful and poignant service, Her Majesty The Queen hosted a reception of some 750 invited guests in the State Apartments at Windsor Castle. Gathering afterwards on the Chapel steps, BBC cameras showed the first glimpse of a smiling Queen welcoming her new daughter in law to the Royal Family.

The younger generation of Royals have taken full advantage of having a Castle at their disposal, enjoying the festive atmosphere of the Castle's great rooms. Prince William

State Visits returned to Windsor Castle with a parade through the town followed by residence and State Dinners in the restored State Apartments.

celebrated his 21st birthday there, attracting more than the usual notoriety when it was famously gate-crashed leading to media outcries for increased security. Princess Beatrice, the eldest daughter of the Duke and Duchess of York, also held a themed costume party at the Castle.

Beefeaters lead the Knights of the Royal Order of the Garter to services at St George's Chapel on Garter Day every June.

A number of high profile royal funerals have also taken place at Windsor Castle since its restoration. On 16 February 2002, the fiftieth anniversary of the burial in St George's Chapel of her father King George VI, Princess Margaret's body was returned to the Castle of her childhood for interment. Her ashes were sealed in the Royal Vault under the Chapel, near his remains. An increasingly isolated figure associated with incessant smoking and an alcohol problem, the once glamorous Princess seemed unable to recover from complications of burns incurred from a dangerously overheated bath. Her funeral and cremation, unusual in the Royal Family, was a relatively low key event with some 450 onlookers. The Royal Family, including the Queen and the Duke of Edinburgh, her children

The Grand Staircase to the Waterloo Chamber sets a medieval tone for visitors. This part of the Castle did not share the same roof as St George's Hall and escaped damage from the fire.

and grandchildren, and Princess Margaret's two children and their father, paid their respects. Poignantly, The Queen Mother was driven from her home at the Royal Lodge in Windsor Great Park to attend her youngest daughter's funeral. Many from the entertainment world, once patronised by a youthful Princess Margaret, also attended. Mourners attended a Castle reception following the service.

It was not long after that the popular Queen Mother joined her husband and her daughter in St George's Chapel. Following the death of her daughter, she appeared to grow increasingly frail. At the age of 101, six weeks after the funeral of the princess, she succumbed to chest infections following a cold. On 30 March 2002, at 3:15 p.m., she died at Royal Lodge in Windsor Great Park with Queen Elizabeth II at her bedside. At the time of her death, she was the longest-lived royal in British history. Mourned as a stalwart representative of the World War II generation, the Queen Mother's funeral was a grand State Occasion. It followed a day of national mourning when more than a million people turned out to pay their respects along the funeral route and many more observed two minutes' silence in the Queen Mother's honour. The coffin was taken from Westminster Hall to Westminster Abbey accompanied by pipers and borne on the same gun carriage used for her husband George VI's funeral 50 years prior. Her funeral service was attended by 2100 guests. Senior members of the Royal Family walked behind the coffin including heirs to the throne Prince

The walls and ceiling of the Waterloo Chamber where the annual Windsor Festival takes place featuring performances by some of the finest orchestras in the country.

Charles, Prince William and Prince Harry. Prince Charles, who had been exceptionally close to his grandmother and often spent time with her as a child when his parents were away on state visits, looked especially stricken. Westminster Abbey's Tenor Bell tolled for every year of the Queen Mother's life. Following the service, The Queen Mother's coffin made the sad return journey to Windsor Castle accompanied by Prince Charles. Hundreds of thousands of onlookers lined the funeral route as the hearse passed by. Senior members of the Royal Family said their final farewells in a private service at St George's Chapel as she took her place beside her husband.

Following the restoration of Windsor Castle and after a long break, the ceremony of State Visits returned to Windsor. Visiting dignitaries were officially received and feted with the full panoply of pageantry followed by state dinners and residence in the State Apartments. These seem to have stopped shortly after 11 September 2001.

Having succeeded in a monumental effort to restore the Castle and the reputation of its sovereign and the royal household, the royal publicity machine has done an excellent job making it more accessible to the media. The medieval archaeological finds following the fire at Windsor prompted a new atmosphere of discovery and Windsor Castle appeared in the news once again. In the summer of 2006, Windsor Castle was one of three royal sites excavated by the *Time Team* of archaeologists led by Tony Robinson. From 25 to 28 August

The Grand Quadrangle looking tranquil. This is where *Time Team* discovered remnants of Edward III's Round Table.

2006, Britain's *Channel 4* covered each day's findings and also followed the royal dig live on *More4*, simulcast on the internet. The Big Royal Dig allowed archaeologists an unprecedented opportunity to uncover new findings over a four-day period with teams working in Buckingham Palace, Holyrood House and Windsor Castle. But it was at Windsor that the most exciting discoveries were made. In the Lower Ward, the Great Hall of Henry III's palace was located with one of its walls still standing. In the Upper Ward, the foundations of the Round Table building erected in 1344 by Edward III were finally discovered. In Edward's day, the Round Table building, 61 metres in diameter, was used for feasting, festivals, and theatrical re-enactments of the Knights of the Round Table of Arthurian legend. The Round Table structure was intended to seat the original 300 Knights of the Garter. Prior to the dig, no one had discovered any proof that it actually existed. Remnants of the building were uncovered by Time Team members in the Castle's Quadrangle – the same Quadrangle which was used by firetrucks and removal vans during the Great Fire. Tony Robinson, the show's presenter, said :

The round table building is one of our most significant ever archaeological finds. It is something that helped to establish Arthurian legends of the Knights of the Round Table. We set out to uncover the walls of the building, and they are just where we hoped. Experts have speculated about the structure for centuries, but they have never been able to find the actual building. We've made discoveries of national importance, which will keep archaeologists and historians busy for years.

All the findings will be catalogued and the survey results added to the Royal archive at Windsor.

Windsor Castle also featured in a BBC programme when its restored Great Kitchen and Staterooms starred in a fly-on-the-wall documentary on the preparations for entertaining at state occasions. All of these increased visitor numbers despite an admission charge. A leading British orchestra is presented in the Waterloo Chamber every year during the Windsor Festival. Since the reopening, and the admission price often includes regular exhibitions of material from The Royal Library at Windsor Castle and Buckingham Palace.

The arched gate to the North Terrace now enlarged to allow fire trucks to pass through should the need arise in the future. You can see the enlargement around the facing.

7
The Restored Monarchy

As Windsor Castle was resurrected and given new life, so too was the British monarchy. The 10th anniversary of the restoration of Windsor Castle, on the 20th November 2007, coincides with the 60th wedding anniversary of Queen Elizabeth II and Prince Philip, the longest marriage in the history of the English throne. In the 55th year of her reign, it is difficult to reconcile Britain's triumphant matriarch with the grim monarch who suffered an "*annus horribilis*" in 1992. She has been able to put behind her the marital troubles of her children as they mature into responsible adults; troublesome ex-spouses have been relegated to mere footnotes in history by untimely death in the case of Princess Diana or public uninterest in the case of the Duchess of York. In poll after poll, her approval rate soars in an unprecedented cross-cultural, cross-generational, multinational cultural phenomenon. She is not just Britain's Queen. She belongs to the world. In "The Queen" she became the sympathetic subject of an Oscar winning Hollywood film seen by millions of moviegoers. In the summer of 2007, she graced the front cover of *Vanity Fair* magazine. Countless television programmes have explored her person and her reign. An awestruck America gave her a royal welcome.

In 2002, the 50th anniversary of her reign was celebrated all year long, culminating in a flawless national spectacle that was reminiscent of an Olympiad. In 2006, her 80th birthday was celebrated twice – on her actual birthday (21 April) with a walkabout in Windsor followed by a family dinner in Windsor Castle, and on her official birthday (17 June). She has successfully negotiated the minefield of public opinion regarding her immediate actions following Princess Diana's tragic death. Where once she was thought to be cold for not

Opposite: The Long Walk from Windsor Castle to the Gates. The Queen and The Royal Family are driven up The Long Walk from Windsor Castle to Ascot Racecourse during Royal Ascot Week.

Queen Elizabeth II
and Prince Philip in
their ceremonial Garter
Robes.

immediately returning to London following the news, she is
now understood to have been concerned about her grandsons
who were staying with her in Balmoral Castle when their
mother's death was discovered. She has seen the heir to the
throne happily married at last. Her divorced second son seems
in no rush to remarry and keeps a low profile. Her youngest has
been sidelined after some complaints that he was exploiting
the Windsor Castle fire by making a video and television
programme. All of her children are now married to what used to
be called 'commoners'. The grandchildren seem well behaved
and scandal free. She has become more accessible to the public,
allowing televised programmes of her royal residences to be
aired. The Monarchy is on the internet.

    During her reign, she has given regular Tuesday evening

audiences to 11 Prime Ministers. A Labour Government, once feared as hell bent on stripping the monarchy of its perks and privileges, proved to be toothless and distracted by war. The Former Prime Minister Tony Blair called the Queen the best of British. The Royal Order of the Garter and the annual Garter ceremony seems steeped in tradition, not a ritual that was only resurrected 60 years ago by her father in the wake of his brother's abdication. Ascot Racecourse has been dramatically rebuilt for a new millennium, a setting fit for the royal ride.

The Queen looks younger than her years and healthy and still does walkabouts in court heels. Although she no longer rides, she remains passionate about horses and horse racing. Since 2005, she has allowed organisers of the annual Royal Windsor Horse Show, which she regularly attends and of which she is patron, to bring the show within Windsor Castle grounds. She walks the corgis in her signature scarf. Her speeches are warm and cordial. Her smile has broadened. She is a queen of quiet confidence in the twenty-first century.

Although her place in history has always been assured, the Great Fire of 1992 at Windsor offered an extraordinary opportunity that had not been foreseen. The Restoration of 1992–1997 has created an enduring architectural legacy in the tradition of Windsor Castle's great historical rebuilding programmes of previous monarchs, assuring that the reign of Queen Elizabeth II will always be an intrinsic part of the fabric of this great building.

A close up of the stained glass window panel honouring the firemen in the Private Chapel created by Joseph Nuttgens based on designs by Prince Philip.

Queen Elizabeth II looking radiant during a State Visit to Windsor Castle by President of Hungary, Arpad Goncz.

Eight
The Post Mortem

Two weeks after the fire, the Berkshire fire services issued their report. Numbering only two pages of A4 text to describe a fire which devastated over one hundred historic rooms and took 44 fire trucks to control, and which also cost the local council alone in excess of £65000, it was quickly branded a whitewash. The report prompted yet more public and press outrage, and national and local calls for an extensive national investigation were heeded. In May of 1993, after a thorough investigation, the Department of National Heritage issued an extensive official report on fire prevention in royal residences by Sir Alan Burleigh with an opening chapter on the Windsor Castle fire and its probable causes, an example that should never be repeated. Although there was no finger pointing, the report begins with the simple statement that there were no fire alarms, fire or smoke detection systems, fire control measures or sprinklers in place in Windsor Castle that day despite the extensive work that was in operation.

The fire was probably started by the halogen spotlights which were three and a half meters above the floor in The Private Chapel on a sliding track about one meter long. The lights and the switching arrangements had been in place since 1976. Unfamiliar with the light system, the restorers working in the Private Chapel turned on all the spotlights, not just a few. It is also possible that a picture stacked on an A-frame was leaning on the curtain, pushing it against the light. Any smouldering that resulted from the contact would have been so high that the smoke would have gone up into the ceiling, making it difficult to detect in the early stages.

Whether the art specialist who first noticed the fire had been informed that there were red phones with direct access to the

Opposite: The Round Tower lit up at night during the annual Royal Windsor Horse show of which the Queen is official Patron.

St George's Chapel is the resting place of ten monarchs and most recently of the Queen Mother and Princess Margaret.

Windsor Castle Fire Brigade will probably never be known. Instead she called the operator at the switchboard, who in turn contacted the firemen, losing valuable minutes. Furthermore, the operator wasn't contacted until after the specialist ran and recruited workman from the adjoining rooms who attempted to fight the flames with available fire extinguishers that couldn't reach the flames. Valuable time was lost. The burning curtain fell to the floor igniting flammable packing materials. Gases rose accumulating in the recesses of lath and plaster.

There were fixed hydraulic hose reels throughout the Castle at the time the fire took place. Yet none were used that day despite the fact that the nearest to the Private Chapel was only 20 metres away.

The greatest contribution to the rapid spread of the fire was the voids behind the panelling, many of which were open for rewiring, and in the ceiling cavities. Behind the

shield on the roof of St George's Hall were vents into the voids.

Other issues came to light. During the fire fighting, radio contact was lost as the communications mast at the top of the Brunswick Tower failed due to the intense heat. Police and firemen were unable to speak to each other and new emergency operations had to be set up at the Windsor Guildhall. This was also the reason that the fire chiefs had to stop operations on two separate occasions when they thought their men were missing, losing more valuable time.

Although the Royal Household took the brunt of the blame from the press, they had in fact only taken over in 1991 after a decade of neglect by the government Property Services Agency.

The Royal Family however had never taken part in any blame game. On the contrary, they were fulsome in their praise of the firemen and salvage workers whose tireless work they had witnessed throughout that day. In a letter sent to the fire services, the Queen declared: "The professionalism, devotion to duty and courage of those who fought the fire have been in the highest tradition of the fire service."

A member of Windsor Castle Fire Brigade maintains watch at their new computerised state of the art Fire Station.

Based on a design by Prince Philip, the stained glass window of the new Private Chapel depicts Windsor Castle surmounting the flames in the upper panel; a rescuer in the salvage operation and a fireman battling the flames flank St George in the lower panel.

Echoing his mother, Prince Charles told the press: " I am convinced that had it not been for the rapid and effective measures taken by the fire service . . . the damage to the castle would have been infinitely worse."

Their profound gratitude has been memorialised in Prince Philip's design for the Stained Glass window in the new Private Chapel. Under a central motif of the Trinity above Windsor Castle are two side panels: one depicting a fireman aiming a hose at the flames, another of a salvage worker carrying a picture from the burning Castle. Six nights before celebrating her 50th wedding anniversary dinner at the restored Castle five years to the day after the fire, a grateful Queen Elizabeth presided over a dinner for 1500 craftsmen & women to thank them in person for making the historic renovation possible.

Astonishing as it now sounds in an age where Health and Safety regulations are so all encompassing, at the time of the Windsor Castle fire, Crown Property was exempt from fire regulations despite the fact that they were open to the public and had staff living quarters. The Windsor Castle fire put a stop to that. Sir Alan Burleigh's report became the benchmark for fire protection for all royal residences.

Windsor Castle now boasts a state of the art fire station and is fully insured.

DISCOVER
Sheffield

Sheena Woodhead & Melvyn Jones

▲ **Hallam University** In the shape of four drums and made from stainless steel, Sheffield Hallam University students' union complex was originally the National Centre for Popular Music.
▼ **Sheaf Square** The dramatic water features on Sheaf Square in front of the city railway station provide a magnificent gateway to Sheffield for those arriving by train.

CONTENTS

MYRIAD

LONDON

The Heart of the City

Sheffield's city centre is dotted with landmarks old and new such as Kemsley House, the Cathedral, the Town Hall, the Lyceum and Crucible theatres and the City Hall. The £130m "Heart of the City" scheme has transformed part of the southern section of the city centre, with the opening of the Millennium Galleries, the Winter Garden, the re-designed Peace Gardens and a new hotel and office block. Soon The Moor, a southern extension of the central retail area, is to be changed out of all recognition by the building of the Sevenstone retail centre between Moorhead, Pinstone Street and Barker's Pool and the relocation of the market quarter from Castlegate to The Moor.

▶ **The Cathedral** The Church of St Peter and St Paul, Sheffield's medieval parish church, became Sheffield cathedral in 1914. The present church initially dates from the early 15th century, replacing an earlier church probably of early 12th century origin. The crossing tower surmounted by its crocketed spire is an important local landmark. The church was restored between 1878-80 by local architects Flockton & Gibbs with advice from Sir George Gilbert Scott. Ambitious 20th-century plans in the inter-war and post-war period to make the church more "cathedral-like" were only partially completed. The most interesting part of the interior is the Shrewsbury Chapel that contains the tombs of the 4th Earl of Shrewsbury (died 1538) lying between his two wives and the 6th Earl of Shrewsbury. In the churchyard is a monument to James Montgomery (1771-1854), newspaper editor and proprietor, campaigner, poet and hymn-writer. He campaigned for many years against slavery and the employment of young children as chimney sweeps and wrote the hymn *Angels from the Realms of Glory*.

◀ **Kemsley House** Among the best-known Sheffield landmarks on High Street (in a reflection, left) is the former *Sheffield Daily Telegraph* building. It was completed in 1916 and is faced with white faience. The portico is surmounted by a statue of Mercury, the Roman god of eloquence, commerce and messenger of the gods.

◀ **Town Hall** Opened in 1897, the Town Hall was described by Sir Nikolaus Pevsner as "a large picturesque pile". (For more on the Town Hall, see page 7.)

▶ **Paradise Square** Behind the Cathedral lies Paradise Square, a throwback to Georgian Sheffield. Built on a sloping cornfield called Hick's Stile Field it dates from 1736-1790. Among its residents in the early 19th century was Sir Francis Chantrey (1781-1841), who as a child was a milkboy bringing milk, butter and eggs for sale from his father's farm in Derbyshire. He became the chosen sculptor of the great and the good of every walk of life. Paradise Square was a popular venue for gatherings and on 15 July, 1779, John Wesley, the founder of Methodism, preached to a large crowd in the square, recording in his diary that it was "the largest congregation I ever saw on a week-day".

▶ **Fargate** Lying at the heart of Sheffield's retail quarter and now pedestrianised, Fargate has an ancient name. "Gate" is from the Old Norse *gata* meaning a street or a lane, so the full name means the furthest extension southwards of the town from the direction of the castle at the junction of the rivers Don and Sheaf, where the town originated in the 12th century.

▶ **The Yorkshire Bank** This five-storey building occupies the corner of Fargate and Surrey Street. It has some carved winged lions and human figures around its balustraded balcony and there are carved gargoyles. The building used to have a temperance restaurant and hotel (the Albany Hotel) on its upper floors. The second particularly interesting building is numbers 38-40 (now WH Smith's) built in the Gothic style in the early 1880s. It was built for Arthur Davy, provisioner, and carries, appropriately enough, above the third floor the carved heads of a sheep, pig, cow and ox, the main constituents of his meat counters.

▲ **Orchard Square** This extension to the central shopping area at the top of Fargate opened in 1987. It is in the form of a courtyard with access to Church Street beyond to the north and Leopold Street to the west. The clocktower in Orchard Square pays homage to Sheffield's industrial past with its working figures of a grinder and a buffer girl.

◀ **Leopold Street** This late Victorian street was named after Prince Leopold, Queen Victoria's youngest son who in 1879 paid an official visit to open Firth College, forerunner of the University of Sheffield, the new building being the square stone building at the far end of the street (right-hand side of the photograph left). Attached to Firth College is what in Edwardian times were the former School Board offices and the Boys' Central Schools. The Central Higher School (opened in 1880) was the first of its kind in the country. The whole block was for many years the City of Sheffield's education offices. Now the building has been transformed into a 90-bedroom luxury hotel, the Leopold, together with a number of restaurants and bars, that opened in 2007.

◀ ▲ **Church Street** To the west of the Cathedral precinct in Church Street stands the Gladstone Buildings built in 1885 as the Reform Club. The second and third floor rooms were the main club rooms and included a dining room, library and lounge. Gothic in style, it is built of red brick with stone dressings, tall mullioned windows, turrets and dormers. Across Church Street stands the Cutlers' Hall, headquarters of the Company of Cutlers in Hallamshire (left) which came into being in 1624. The present hall, in Grecian style with four Corinthian columns, was the third hall to be built for the Cutlers and was completed in 1832 and extended in 1888. Church Street is a busy route for the Supertram system. This was completed between 1994 and 1995 with routes extending to Middlewood and Malin Bridge in the north, Halfway, Herdings and Crystal Peaks in the south-east and Meadowhall Shopping Centre in the east.

The City Hall Opened in 1932, the City Hall was originally designed as early as 1920, by E Vincent Harris, but construction did not begin until 1929. It has been completely refurbished at a cost of over £12m. Constructed from stone quarried in Darley Dale, Derbyshire, it is in the Classical Revival style dominated by a portico with eight Corinthian columns. Originally conceived as a memorial hall to the city's First World War dead it became Sheffield's main concert hall with a memorial hall (right) at the rear. The main hall accommodates 2,800 people.

Barker's Pool This open space in front of the City Hall has a most interesting history. Lying beyond the end of Fargate in the medieval period was an area known as Balm Green which contained Barker's Pool, which really was a pool, a source of fresh water to supplement the supply from public and private wells until 1793. Details of minor improvements made to Barker's Pool survive from as early as 1572 when it was walled, "feyed" (ie cleaned) and a new bolt was fixed to the shuttle. The shuttle (a sluice gate) would have been an important feature when water from the pool was occasionally released and channelled through the town to clean its streets, eventually finding its way down into the river Don. The pool also contained at one period the town's "cucking stool", for ducking women and other objectionable persons who spread malicious gossip!

Ceremonial Since 1925 Barker's Pool has been the venue for a memorial service on Remembrance Day, and in 1945 it was the scene of jubilant celebrations to mark the end of the war in Europe (VE Day). Now every year in late November it is full of students and their families during Sheffield Hallam University's degree conferment ceremony in the City Hall. When the City Hall was recently refurbished Barker's Pool was re-paved and two new fountains were installed.

War Memorial This memorial, to the 5,000 men who died in the First World War, was unveiled in 1925 and arose from a competition announced a year earlier. The competition was won by CD Carus Wilson, head of the University of Sheffield's School of Architecture. It is in the form of a steel pole rising 90ft (27m) from a bronze base. The pole is surrounded by the life-size figures of four soldiers sculpted by George Alexander.

Town Hall The centre of Sheffield is dominated by the Town Hall, built of Derbyshire sandstone, standing at the junction of Surrey Street and Pinstone Street. Designed by EW Mountford, it was opened by Queen Victoria in 1897. After opening the Town Hall she was driven to Norfolk Park where 50,000 children had been assembled to sing to the queen. The visit ended with a trip to Charles Cammell's Cyclops steelworks. Reflecting Sheffield's industrial history there are two friezes carved in stone around the exterior walls of the Town Hall which depict, among other things, grinders, smiths, smelters and miners. The 200ft tower is surmounted by an 8ft high bronze statue of Vulcan, the Roman god of fire and furnaces, with his right foot on an anvil and pincers in his left hand. Inside is a life-size statue of the Duke of Norfolk and a bust of Queen Victoria.

Peace Gardens These gardens in Sheffield's most central civic space occupy the site of St Paul's Church. This church was begun in 1720 but did not open until 1740. This was because of an argument between the donor of £10,000 for its construction, John Downes, a goldsmith, and the church authorities, about the right of appointment of a curate. The church was demolished in 1937. The site was cleared in the same year to make a public open space named to commemorate the peace expected from the Munich agreement of 1938. The gardens were redesigned in 1997-98 as part of the "Heart of the City" project. An interesting feature of the newly-designed space are bronze vessels from which water overflows and runs down tiled cascades. They are said to represent the rivers on which Sheffield's early prosperity was based.

The Winter Garden This is the green heart of Sheffield, the crowning glory of the £120m "Heart of the City" project. It is a place for office workers and shoppers to meet or relax and combines stunning architecture with a unique collection of plants. The new structure was opened in December 2002 with a children's candlelight procession and fireworks and within a year it had attracted more than 1m visitors. It is 230ft (70m) long and 72ft (22m) wide and its arched structure is formed by 10 pairs of parabolic wooden arches that reach up to 72ft (22m). Made of larch, the arches require no preservative coatings and will mature to a silvery grey colour. The Winter Garden is a temperate glasshouse with the temperature kept constant, frost kept at bay and humidity closely controlled. This is achieved in a number of ways. The building is glazed with more than 1,400 glass panels of which 128 open and close automatically. Fans move concentrations of hot air in summer which is then released through the vents. Underfloor heating protects the plants from frost and small water features control levels of humidity. The Winter Garden houses 2,500 plants of over 150 species mainly from the Southern Hemisphere including palms from Madagascar, grasses and trees from Australia and pines from Norfolk Island. Most of the plants bloom in winter – hence the name Winter Garden!

Tudor Square Lying at the centre of Sheffield's cultural life, Tudor Square is bounded on the north by the Crucible Theatre, on the south by the entrance to the Winter Garden, on the east by the Lyceum Theatre (below) and the Central Library and Graves Art Gallery (left) and on the west by bars and restaurants. The Crucible Theatre, built in 1969-70, is not very eye-catching from the outside, but inside things are very different. The auditorium has a central thrust stage almost surrounded by banks of seating for an audience of 1,000. Under the same roof, the Crucible Studio Theatre holds an audience of 400 people completely in the round. The Central Library and Graves Art Gallery, in Portland stone, were built between 1929 and 1934. The Graves Art Gallery was the gift of Alderman JG Graves who also donated 400 paintings and drawings.

The Lyceum Theatre Built in 1893 as the City Theatre, it was partially destroyed in a fire in 1896, and under new ownership was re-modelled in 1897 by the theatre architect WGR Sprague. The Lyceum is thought to be the only surviving example of Sprague's work outside London. The exterior of the theatre has stucco decoration and a corner dome surmounted by a figure of Mercury. But it was the interior of the theatre, the auditorium, that was magnificent. The walls were covered in fine plasterwork, cherubs separated painted panels, the proscenium arch was surrounded by rococo plasterwork, above was a beautiful ceiling and all was lit by the most advanced form of gas lighting. The theatre was sympathetically restored, inside and out in 1989-90. It is now the venue for West End touring productions, operas by Opera North and local productions.

Millennium Galleries Completed in 2001 as part of the "Heart of the City" project, the Millennium Galleries have three complementary roles. First and foremost they extend the city's museum space by nearly 2,000 square metres; together with the adjoining Winter Garden, they form an interesting covered section on the route from the railway station and Sheffield Hallam University to the urban centre; and the Azure café is a pleasant space in which to have a refreshing drink or snack. The Millennium Galleries face onto Arundel Gate with the café on the ground floor. The galleries occupy the upper floor and are reached from Arundel Gate by escalator. Along with temporary exhibitions there is a permanent space for Sheffield's metalwork and silverware collection and the Ruskin Collection. This the property of the Guild of St George, an organisation set up by John Ruskin to broaden the minds of working people, that established its first museum in Sheffield in 1875.

Fitzalan Square So-called after one of the family names of the Dukes of Norfolk, the major private landowner in Sheffield, Fitzalan Square was laid out over a protracted period from 1869 to 1881. Early 20th century photographs of the square show it as an important tram terminus crowded with waiting horse cabs. At its centre is a bronze statue of King Edward VII dating from 1913 by Alfred Drury. On the pedestal are scenes representing Philanthropy, Peace and Unity. The Philanthropy scene shows human figures holding aloft a model of the King Edward VII Hospital.

Victoria Hall A striking building on Norfolk Street is the Methodist Victoria Hall. Built in brick and stone in a mixture of Gothic and Arts & Crafts styles it was completed in 1908. It has a tall square tower with a large Baroque top and interesting carved decoration, including carvings of John and Charles Wesley. The hall has recently undergone a thorough refurbishment. The first phase completed in 2005 included a new reception area, lifts and easier access for visitors with mobility problems. The second phase included cleaning the facade, creating a new lounge at the rear of the worship room and opening a new café.

▶ **Castle House** This large store, standing at the junction of Angel Street and Castle Street, was built between 1959 and 1964 for Brightside and Carbrook Co-operative Society. It was also the society's headquarters. It replaced an early large store on Exchange Street that was very badly damaged during the Blitz of 1940. Castle House was the Sheffield Co-operative Society's department store until the spring of 2008. An unusual feature of the store is the spiral staircase, cantilevered, with banisters of stainless steel leading to a glass dome. On the wall facing King Street is a figure representing Vulcan, the Roman god of fire, whose most ancient festival was the Fornacalia, held in his honour as god of furnaces. He holds a special place in the history of Sheffield, once known as "Steel City" and also appears on top of the Town Hall as an 8ft high bronze statue.

▼ **Sheffield Hallam University** This is one of the "new" universities created in 1992 from Sheffield City Polytechnic. Until the 1970s there were a number of colleges in the Sheffield region, each with their own culture and ethos. On the Pond Street site, now the City Campus, was the College of Technology that was created in 1950 and which occupied an expanding site built between 1953 and 1968. In 1969 the College of Technology merged with the College of Art which occupied a site on Psalter Lane two miles to the south-west of the city centre, to form Sheffield Polytechnic. The varied origins and specialisms of its component parts has meant that Sheffield Hallam University, from its outset, has been able to offer a wide range of undergraduate and postgraduate degree courses. It prides itself on its close links with employers, and a greater percentage of students than at any other British university are on courses with a work placement.

Around the Heart of the City

In the 19th and the first half of the 20th century the areas around Sheffield city centre consisted of streets of back-to-back and terraced housing. Most of this has now been demolished and replaced by tower blocks and other high-rise developments. In recent years city centre living has become popular and new apartment blocks have been built on old industrial sites, especially along waterfronts, and disused factories and warehouses converted to residential use. Major sporting venues such as Ponds Forge International Leisure Centre and Bramall Lane football ground also lie close to the city centre.

▶ Park Hill Flats High above the Sheaf valley stand the Park Hill flats, Sheffield's "streets in the sky". These flats, acclaimed by architects and sociologists in their early days, have also been referred to by other experts as extreme examples of Sixties' architectural brutalism. They are now Grade II (starred) listed and a refurbishment scheme has been agreed to transform the complex into upmarket apartments, rented flats and small business premises. Below are the Hyde Park flats that stand to the north of the Park Hill flats overlooking the confluence of the Don and Sheaf. They are the re-clad two remaining tower blocks of the original three. Completed in 1966, the central block was demolished in 1992 and the two remaining blocks were taken back to their concrete frameworks and re-clad in red and yellow brick. Behind the re-clad blocks can just be seen the spire of St John's church (1836-38) which originally stood among tightly-packed back-to-back houses.

◀ ▼ Railway Station Sheffield did not get a direct railway route to London until 1870 when the first station on this site was built. Before then a railway journey to London involved a trip to Rotherham on the Sheffield and Rotherham Railway, then a train on the Midland Railway's line from York to London via Derby. This was to avoid the broad ridge between Sheffield and Chesterfield to the south that would have required very deep cuttings. Instead George Stephenson took the line to Rotherham through the Rother valley where the gradients were easier. The 1870 line to Chesterfield breaches the high ridge via the Bradway tunnel. The present station, still known to many as the "Midland Station", is the creation of Charles Trubshaw in 1905; some of the 1870 station still survives on platform 2.

Sheaf Square Visitors arriving in Sheffield by train in the last few years have seen tremendous changes. Not only has the station itself been refurbished but the townscape outside has been transformed. Gone is the roundabout at the bottom of Howard Street, the office blocks of Sheaf House and Dyson House have been demolished, the line of Sheaf Street has been re-aligned and immediately in front of the station a new public square, Sheaf Square, has been created. This has water features, trees and public seating. On the edge of the square beside Sheaf Street is a stainless steel sculpture – the Cutting Edge. The sculpture and the station façade are all illuminated at night. Stainless steel was a Sheffield invention in 1913. The discoverer of stainless steel, a chromium steel that almost completely resists corrosion, was Harry Brearley. Locally-born (in Ramsden's Yard, off the Wicker) he rose from being a bottle-washer to director of Brown-Firth's research laboratories.

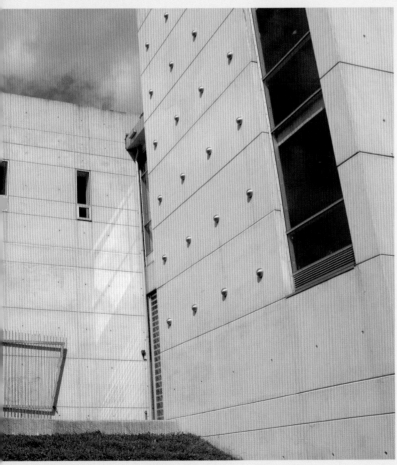

▲ **SHU Students' Union Building** This building is peculiarly shaped because it was the short-term home of the National Centre for Popular Music. It is in the shape of four drums of stainless steel, each drum tilted outwards. Funded by a large Lottery grant, it was completed in 1998. The Centre for Popular Music had a short life and after lying vacant for a time it was acquired in 2003 by Sheffield Hallam University for use as the students' union building. It now contains a ground-floor public bar serving hot foods and snacks throughout the day, a shop and a student bar, as well as meeting rooms for clubs and societies. The exterior is polished about once a year.

◄ **The Persistence Works** Located on Brown Street, the Persistence Works is a new building that contains studios for craftspeople and artists, members of the Yorkshire Artspace Society (YAS). Constructed from concrete it consists of a low block with a six-storey block behind and was completed in 2001; it incorporated seven artists' commissions in its design. Brown Street is located in an area to the south-east of the city centre that has now been designated as the Cultural Industries Quarter. Originally laid out in the late 18th century and subsequently occupied by cutlers' workshops and metalworking businesses the area has now been colonised by small and medium-sized enterprises in the arts, communications and media.

Bramall Lane Lying immediately to the south of the city centre, Bramall Lane is the home of Sheffield United, the "Blades". Yorkshire County Cricket Club was founded in Sheffield in 1863 and County matches were played at Bramall Lane for more than a century. It became Sheffield United's football ground in 1889. The Blades were the Football League Division 1 Champions in 1897-98 only seven years after being elected to Division 2. Their early record in the FA Cup is outstanding: they were winners in 1899, 1902, 1915 and 1925 and runners-up in 1901 and 1936.

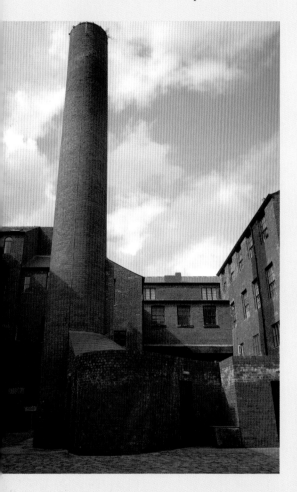

Devonshire Green The now fashionable Devonshire Quarter between the city centre and the University of Sheffield is a part of the inner city that has seen the development of some large-scale residential building in recent years. The green itself was a bombed part of the city during the Second World War that was never built on again and which has now been transformed into a modern public open space with colourful planting. To the west of the green (in the background) is the prestigious West One development consisting of 500 apartments with restaurants, cafés and bars.

The Somme Barracks Dating from 1907 the Somme Barracks were built for the West Yorkshire Royal Engineers Volunteers. The gatehouse has a high and wide arched doorway below a tower with a mullioned and transom window and above that the name, then the royal coat of arms before reaching the top surmounted by two small turrets. Further along West Street are the Cavendish Buildings which also date from 1907. They were built as a garage and showroom for the Sheffield Motor Company. The faience-covered three-storey façade has mullioned windows and the roofline is broken by four elaborate pediments with the building's dates.

Butcher's Wheel In 1893, White's Sheffield Directory listed 281 table knife manufacturers, 125 scissors-makers, and 128 electro-plate and nickel-silver makers. Butcher's Wheel on Arundel Street is one of the best of the few still surviving Victorian cutlery, edge tool and file-making works in Sheffield. This brick-built works extending to four storeys was constructed in the mid-19th century by William and Samuel Butcher. Unused for a long time and recently refurbished it still manages to exude a sense of Dickensian working conditions. The large first and second floor casements were designed to shed maximum light on the "grinding hulls" that occupied those floors.

▶ ▼ The University of Sheffield Officially opened by King Edward VII on 12 July 1905, the new university had started life as a university college in 1897, being an amalgamation of Firth College (which became the School of Arts & Science), the Medical Institution (which became the Medical School) and the Technical School (which became the School of Technology). The commitment to gain full university status had been spurred on when it was mooted that the University College of Leeds should become the University of Yorkshire. The new red brick university buildings, Firth Court (below), at Western Bank beside Weston Park, were designed by Mitchell Gibbs in the Tudor style. Dominating the Western Bank campus today is the 21-storey Arts Tower, which was completed in 1965. Considerable refurbishment is now planned. The building currently contains two conventional lifts and a "paternoster" lift. The latter, open-doored and in continual motion up and down, is said to have deterred some prospective students from taking up the place offered to them! The University of Sheffield, which has 26,000 students, has an enviable reputation. In 2001 it won *The Sunday Times* University of the Year award and was described by *The Times* as one of the powerhouses of British higher education.

▶ Cornish Place Works

Viewed from Ball Street Bridge, this was the factory of James Dixon & Sons, manufacturer of silverware, silver plate and Britannia metal goods. Founded in 1805, the firm moved to Cornish Place in 1822. At the beginning of the 20th century James Dixon had a workforce of more than 900 but by the 1990s the firm had ceased to exist and the works were converted into apartments in 1998. Ball Street Bridge (right) was re-built after the Great Sheffield Flood of 11 March 1864 that caused the death of 240 people. The bridge collapsed from the weight of the machinery and timber brought down by flood water that battered its arches.

◀ **Cementation Furnace** Until the second half of the 18th century the steel used by Sheffield's cutlers was either imported or was locally made "shear steel" which was forged from "blister steel" made in a cementation furnace. Some 260 such furnaces, easily recognised by their conical chimneys, were eventually built in Sheffield, of which only one survives, on Hoyle Street (left). Alternate layers of charcoal and iron bars covered by a layer of mortar were placed in two sandstone chests inside a cementation furnace. The furnace was sealed and a coal fire lit below the chests which burned for seven to nine days. The iron bars now converted to blister steel (they were covered in small blisters) were then made into shear steel by being heated in bundles to bright red and then forged into a uniform bar.

▶ **Kelham Island Industrial Museum** Opened in 1982, the museum, which tells the story of Sheffield's industrial development, occupies the old electricity generating station for the electric tramway system. The visitor is greeted by the sight of a Bessemer converter. The Bessemer converter made its first appearance on Carlisle Street at Bessemer's Steel Works in 1858. This was a radical step by its inventor Henry Bessemer since the new invention was greeted with scepticism by the rather conservative Sheffield steel producers who were doubtful about the quality of the large amounts of steel that were produced in a short space of time. Bessemer, the outsider, saw his new works initially as a place of demonstration for potential licensees. Two of Sheffield's major firms, John Brown's and Charles Cammell's, became the earliest converts and produced their first Bessemer steel rails in 1861, followed by Samuel Fox in 1863.

▲ **Aizlewood's Mill** The Don valley to the north-west of the city centre has a mixture of newbuilds and refurbished industrial buildings. Aizlewood's Mill (the Crown Flour Mills) is located on Nursery Street north of the river Don. Standing six storeys high with a tall rectangular-shaped chimney, the mill has now been converted into offices and workshops.

◀▶ **Victoria Quays** In the 17th and 18th centuries, Sheffield's steel products were transported by packhorse to the ports of Yorkshire and Lancashire. Goods for the London and European market went to the river port of Bawtry where they were transferred to barges and carried down the river Idle to the Trent and the port of Hull. The inconvenience and slowness of the overland journey from Sheffield to Bawtry led the Cutlers Company to explore the possibility of making the Don navigable from Doncaster to Sheffield and in 1726 an Act of Parliament was passed and work began. But it proved impracticable to extend the waterway and so Tinsley remained the terminus from 1751 until 1819 when the Sheffield canal opened, terminating at the Canal Basin near the junction of the Sheaf and Don. The extension of the canal into Sheffield was greeted with acclaim and a fleet of barges with flags and bands made a triumphal entry into the Canal Basin. The Basin was refurbished, renamed the Victoria Quays and opened by the Prince of Wales in 1994. Shown here are the restored Coal Merchants' Offices (left) and the Straddle Warehouse (right).

The Suburbs

The pre-twentieth century residential and industrial suburbs of Sheffield were largely in the outlying townships of the former medieval parish – to the west in Nether Hallam and Upper Hallam, to the south and south-west in Ecclesall and in the east and north-east in Attercliffe cum Darnall and Brightside. Norton was annexed from Derbyshire in 1901, Stannington was incorporated gradually between 1901 and 1914, Handsworth in 1920, and Dore and Totley, like Norton formerly part of Derbyshire, between 1929 and 1934. In 1967 another part of Derbyshire, Mosborough, became part of the city and after the reorganisation of local government in 1974 the former West Riding County Council communities of Bradfield, Stocksbridge, Oughtibridge, Worrall, Grenoside, High Green, Chapeltown and Ecclesfield became part of Sheffield.

Below, the Gleadless Valley, built in the 1950s and 1960s, one of the biggest public housing developments in the country.

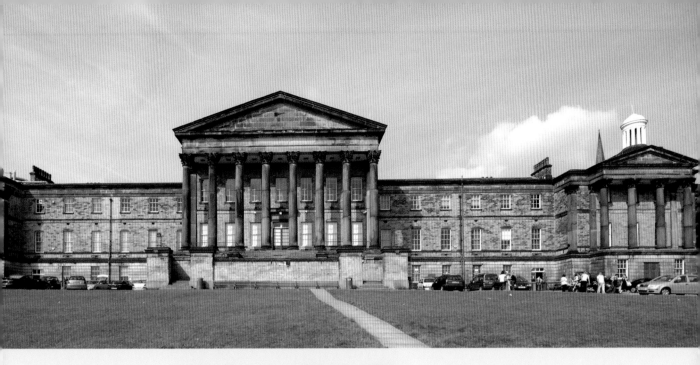

▲ King Edward VII School
Designed by William
Flockton (born 1804) and
built between 1837-40 as the
Wesley Proprietary Grammar
School, later the Wesley
College, this handsome
school is known to locals as
"King Ted's". With his
partners and his son,
Thomas, Flockton designed
a number of fine buildings in
Sheffield. These include the
New Chapel in the General
Cemetery, Kenwood, the
home of George Wostenholm,
cutlery manufacturer and the
houses of three of Sheffield's
most successful steel
magnates: Tapton Hall, for
Edward Vickers, Oakbrook
for Sir John Brown and
Endcliffe Hall for Mark Firth.

▲ ◄ Norton Church Norton was part of
Derbyshire until 1901 and the centre still has
a village atmosphere with its obelisk to the
sculptor, Sir Francis Chantrey, who was born
in the parish, its war memorial, the rectory and
the medieval church. The church, St James', is
a combination of styles: the exterior is mainly
Perpendicular but it includes a restored
Norman south doorway and a mainly Early
English tower. Inside the church there is a fine
early 16th century alabaster monument of
William Blythe and his wife. It is said that it
was the Blythe tomb in Norton church that
kindled Chantrey's interest in sculpture.

▼ Sharrow Snuff Mill The water-powered
site on the river Porter occupied by Wilson's
Sharrow Snuff Mill has been in operation since
at least the late 16th century. A new snuff mill
was built in 1763 and has been run by the
Wilson family ever since. By the early 19th
century the waterwheel was joined by a steam
engine in the production process. Although
no longer used in snuff production, the whole
water-power system is still in place: a weir on the
river Porter deflects the water to the building.

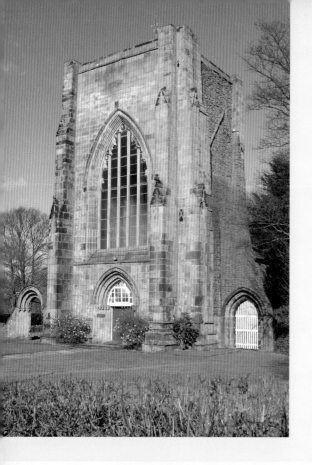

◄ **Beauchief Abbey** Formerly in that part of north Derbyshire that became part of Sheffield in 1901, the name "Beauchief" is Norman-French and means "beautiful headland". It is pronounced "Bee-chif". The abbey was founded between 1173 and 1176 by Robert Fitzranulf, lord of the manor of Norton and Alfreton, for the Premonstratensians who were known as the White Canons and were noted for founding their monastic houses in isolated locations and living in poverty.

▼ **Abbeydale Industrial Hamlet** This is the best preserved water-powered industrial site in Sheffield and is managed by the Sheffield Industrial Museums Trust. The works were the site of a scythemaking business from 1714 until 1935 and before that there is circumstantial evidence that it was a lead-smelting mill. The method of harnessing water power, clearly exemplified at Abbeydale, was that a weir was built to deflect water from the river, in this case the river Sheaf, into a reservoir, locally called a dam, via a channel called a goit or leat. By the end of the 18th century there were 130 water-powered sites on Sheffield's rivers.

Dore & Totley Travel just a short distance up the A621 (Baslow Road) beyond the post office in Totley and you are in the Peak District National Park. Now a busy suburb in south Sheffield, Totley, like its neighbour Dore (left), was until the late 1920s part of north Derbyshire. The most historic part of the village is still characterised by cottages and farmsteads built of the warm local gritstone. Perhaps the oldest building in the village is Totley Old Hall, parts of which date from 1623 (there is a datestone above the doorway) but there were substantial alterations and additions in the Victorian period. The last private owner was William Aldam Milner who lived there from the 1880s until his death in 1931. The Hall has since been converted into apartments.

▼ **Ringinglow Roundhouse** This tollhouse, the best-known surviving tollhouse in Sheffield, was located at a junction on the turnpike road system where the roughly east-west Sheffield-Hathersage-Chapel-en-le-Frith road met the road turning south to the Fox Inn and on towards Buxton. By the 18th century road traffic was increasing so much that the ancient system of parishes or townships being responsible for the maintenance of highways within their jurisdiction could not cope. The system of turnpikes therefore came into being on which tolls were charged at tollgates. The roundhouse at Ringinglow is actually octagonal in shape and allowed the toll-keeper to have clear views of traffic approaching the gates in all directions. The roundhouse operated as a toll-keeper's house from 1795 to 1825.

▲ **Fulwood Old Chapel** This Unitarian place of worship is simple but appealing and dates from 1728. Money to build "a large and handsome Chapel" was left in the will of Fulwood resident William Ronksley. It has an adjoining schoolroom and at the rear is the old Chapel House where the minister once resided. In the chapel garden are the old village stocks.

▶ Ecclesfield Church

St Mary's church, Ecclesfield was largely rebuilt between 1480 and 1520. It stands on the site of a much earlier Christian shrine that gave the original village its name. The name Ecclesfield means an open space in an otherwise well-wooded area ("field"), in which stood a Christian church (*ecclesia*). In the churchyard is buried Alexander John Scott (1768-1840), Nelson's chaplain at Trafalgar.

▼ Hillsborough Barracks

Located between Langsett Road and Penistone Road in Hillsborough, Hillsborough Barracks were built in the early 1850s following the Chartist demonstrations of the 1840s. Originally the barracks included quarters for officers and their servants, a chapel, a hospital, infantry soldiers' quarters, cavalry soldiers' quarters and a school for 80 children.

▼ Hillsborough Football Ground The home ground of Sheffield Wednesday FC, nicknamed "The Owls". The club was founded in 1867 as the football side of Wednesday Cricket Club. After playing in different locations, Hillsborough became the club's ground in 1899, but did not take its modern name of Hillsborough until 1914. The record attendance at the ground was nearly 73,000 in 1934. The capacity of today's all-seater stadium is nearly 40,000. Wednesday have a fine League and Cup record, being Division 1 champions in 1902-03, 1903-04, 1928-29 and 1929-30 and FA Cup winners in 1896, 1907 and 1935.

▶ Hallam FC Sandygate's main claim to fame is that it is the home of Hallam FC. Founded on 4 September 1860, Hallam FC is recognised as being one of the oldest football clubs in the world. This honour does not quite match the fame of its close rival Sheffield FC which is the oldest football club in the world, having been founded in 1857. Hallam FC still play at the same ground, on Sandygate Road, Crosspool, which according to the *Guinness Book of Records* is the oldest football ground in the world.

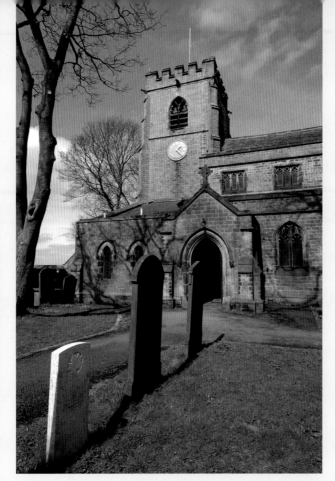

◀ **Bolsterstone** This small Pennine village lies at nearly 1000ft (306m) between the industrial town of Stocksbridge to the north and Broomhead and More Hall reservoirs in the Ewden valley to the south. The village is home to the famous Bolsterstone Male Voice Choir. Founded in 1934, the nucleus of the new choir came from the church choir.

▼ **Stocksbridge Clock Tower** Stocksbridge was a Victorian industrial community created around Samuel Fox's steelworks. Fox amassed fortunes from umbrella frames and steel rails. Built between 1920 and 1923 as a war memorial, the Clock Tower's construction was funded by public sub-scription and built on land granted by RHR Rimington Wilson of nearby Broomhead Hall.

▲ **St James' Chapel, Midhopestones** Perched above the Little Don valley to the west of Stocksbridge (formerly on the northern edge of the extensive ancient parish of Ecclesfield), is St James' Chapel in the village of Midhopestones. The "hop" in Midhopestones means a small enclosed valley as in Glossop and Worksop. The medieval chapel-of-ease that existed here was re-built in 1705 by Godfrey Bosville, as the initials and date on the wall show. Bosville was the lord of the manor and resided at Gunthwaite Hall six miles (10 km) to the north where he also had a deer park. The chapel is a tiny building constructed of local gritstone with a stone slate roof. It has plain mullioned windows and a small bell turret with a pyramidal top. Inside there is a Jacobean pulpit. The chapel still contains the original pews and the west gallery built by Bosville.

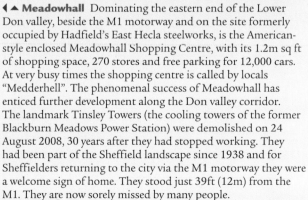

◀ ▲ **Meadowhall** Dominating the eastern end of the Lower Don valley, beside the M1 motorway and on the site formerly occupied by Hadfield's East Hecla steelworks, is the American-style enclosed Meadowhall Shopping Centre, with its 1.2m sq ft of shopping space, 270 stores and free parking for 12,000 cars. At very busy times the shopping centre is called by locals "Medderhell". The phenomenal success of Meadowhall has enticed further development along the Don valley corridor. The landmark Tinsley Towers (the cooling towers of the former Blackburn Meadows Power Station) were demolished on 24 August 2008, 30 years after they had stopped working. They had been part of the Sheffield landscape since 1938 and for Sheffielders returning to the city via the M1 motorway they were a welcome sign of home. They stood just 39ft (12m) from the M1. They are now sorely missed by many people.

◄ Lower Don Valley Industry For 120 years the Lower Don valley was the city's industrial heartland. This powerhouse of industry was laid waste by the recession of the early 1980s. Sheffield Forgemasters (left), created from the merging of some of the most famous names in the industry, managed to keep its head above water and now is a prosperous concern.

▼ River Don Works The offices of Vickers' River Don works, dating from 1906, once the hub of a mighty business concern, now lie empty and for sale. The firm was founded by Sheffield-born Edward Vickers who took over the steel firm of Naylor, Vickers & Co at Millsands in 1867 and moved to the River Don Works in Brightside. The firm manufactured steel, armaments, ships and aircraft parts.

◄ Leisure and sports facilities
Three sporting arenas have made important contributions to the regeneration of the Lower Don valley: the Don Valley Stadium, the largest athletics stadium in the UK; the English Institute of Sport which provides state-of-the-art facilities and support services for world-class athletes, and iceSheffield (left) which contains two Olympic-size ice rinks and seating for 1,500 spectators. The nearby Arena holds 12,000 people and hosts concerts by international pop stars. It is the home of Sheffield Steelers ice hockey team. Described by various architectural writers as "hulking", "dreary" and "dull" it was opened in 1991 for the World Student Games. The bridge over Coleridge Road that links the Arena with iceSheffield and the Don Valley Stadium is an attractive addition to the Lower Don valley landscape.

Sheffield's Urban Countryside

Sheffield is blessed with an enormous variety of green spaces plus its own "lake district" to the west and north-west of the city where the valleys are occupied by reservoirs. The city's "heritage" public parks such as the Botanical Gardens, Norfolk Park, Firth Park, Weston Park, Endcliffe Park, Meersbrook Park, Hillsborough Park and Whiteley Woods were enriched in the 20th century with the acquisition of Millhouses Park, Graves Park and Whirlow Brook Park. The 80 ancient woodlands dotted about the city add a further dimension to the city's green attractions.

◀ ▼ The Botanical Gardens
Opened in 1836 (but only to shareholders and subscribers except on special occasions until 1898) the Botanical Gardens were designed by Robert Marnock who, in 1840, became curator of the Royal Botanical Gardens in Regent's Park, London. Covering 19 acres, the gardens were restored with the help of a Lottery Fund award of £5m in 1997. The photographs on these pages show the gatehouse at the entrance to the gardens (below) and the restored glass pavilions (left). The garden has a restored bear pit which was home to two live bears until the 1870s.

◀ Weston Park was created from the grounds of Weston Hall, an early 19th century house built by Thomas Harrison, an eminent Sheffield sawmaker. His two daughters inherited the Weston Hall estate and on their death it was bought by Sheffield Corporation for £18,000. The grounds were re-designed as a public park by Robert Marnock. The hall became Sheffield's first museum. It was rebuilt in 1935 and has recently undergone extensive refurbishment funded by the Heritage Lottery Fund. The park and museum were officially opened in September 1875. The *Sheffield Daily Telegraph* reported that the park "was thronged by a well-behaved and highly delighted crowd. The weather was fine. The park looked in its gayest summer dress". By the 1980s and 1990s this strategically located park (it lies next to the University of Sheffield and the Children's Hospital) had become very neglected but a Lottery Fund award has allowed it to benefit from a much needed facelift.

▼ **Meersbrook Park** The land on which Meersbrook Park stands was purchased by Sheffield Corporation in 1886 to prevent it from being acquired for housing and to provide something more than just a place in which to promenade. Originally it included an ornamental rose garden, and a rockery with a cascade walk in an area known as The Glen, crossed by a rustic bridge. But these attractions have now mostly been lost. However the park is still handsome, with wonderful views across the city (below) and a walled garden that provides training and volunteering opportunities.

▶ **Bishops' House Museum** Tucked away at the top of Meersbrook Park, this is the best surviving timber-framed house in Sheffield. Built about 1500 for a yeoman farmer-scythemaker, its interior contains many of its original features and looks just as it would have done in the 17th century, giving a flavour of life in Stuart England. The wonderful timber work can be examined at close quarters, inside and out. From the leafy Meersbrook Park there are stunning views across the entire city to the north. The park boasts a second historic building – Meersbrook House, built in 1780 by Benjamin Roebuck.

◀ ▲ ▼ **Hillsborough Park** This park was originally the grounds of Hillsborough House, built in 1779 for Thomas Steade. In the 19th century it was successively in the ownership of John Rodgers of Joseph Rodgers & Sons, cutlery manufacturers, and the Dixon family, of the silverware and silver-plating company. Sheffield Corporation bought Hillsborough Park (excluding the hall) in 1890 and opened it as a public park in 1892. In 1903 the hall was also purchased and opened as a branch library. The lake in the park, an enlarged version of the original lake, was used for boating until about 1960. It is now a haven for wildlife and is used for fishing. A special feature of the park is the former walled kitchen garden. Work to restore this garden was begun by volunteers in 1991. It was re-opened by the Duke of Kent on 15 April 1993, the anniversary of the Hillsborough Stadium disaster in which 96 football supporters died. A Memorial Garden in the walled garden commemorates their lives.

▲ **Whirlow Brook Park** Lying four miles to the south-west of the city centre is the Limb valley with Whirlow Brook Park at its southern end. Whirlow Brook Park was purchased by the Town Trustees and the JG Graves Charitable Trust in 1946 and presented to the city. It was opened to the public in June 1951. Whirlow Brook House was built in 1906 by Mr and Mrs Percy Fawcett. Mr Fawcett's sister and husband, Mr and Mrs Walter Benton Jones, moved into the house in 1920 and invited the Royal Horticultural Society to advise on planting and planning the grounds during the late 1920s. The gardens that were created, so typical of the time, remain just about intact. There is a rock garden constructed of millstone grit, two pools and a lower lake. The house is now a restaurant. Continuing up the valley the path leads through mixed woodlands and eventually into much more open ground with young birch and hawthorn and wet pastureland and heath. The stream is boulder-strewn and most attractive.